BRUM
AND
BRUMMIES

Volume 2

Unless otherwise stated all photographs are from the archives of the Birmingham *Evening Mail*. I thank the Mail for allowing them to be used.

BRUM
AND
BRUMMIES

Volume 2

Carl Chinn

**BREWIN
BOOKS**

First published in 2001 by
Brewin Books, Studley, Warwickshire B80 7LG

© Carl Chinn 2001

British Library Cataloguing in Publication Data
A catalogue record for this book is available from
The British Library

ISBN: 1 85858 202 4

Typeset in Times and made and printed
in Great Britain by Warwick Printing Company Limited,
Theatre Street, Warwick, Warwickshire CV34 4DR.

CONTENTS

Chapter 1   **The Heart of Brum: The Bull Ring**

The Bull Ring of Memory: The Old Bull Ring   1
The Street of Barrow Boys: Spiceal Street   5
The Thrill of Market Day   11
A Wondrous Building: The Old Market Hall   15
Custodian of the Soul of Brum: Saint Martin's   20
Honoured First in Brum: Nelson's Statue   24
At the Heart of Things: Brum's Barrow Boys   28
Laying the Wreath: The End of the Old Bull Ring   32
A Vision of America: The 1960s Bull Ring   36

Chapter 2   **Brummies**

Brummies Helping Themselves:
    The Birmingham Hospital Saturday Fund   41
A Woman Who Gave: Elizabeth Green and Her Mission   45
The Gentleman Champion from Ashted: Jack Hood   48
Labouring for the Rights of Workers: Brummie Trade Unionists   52
A Hero of the Great War: Arthur Vickers VC   56

Chapter 3   **The Old End**

Beyond the Edge of the World: Billesley   61
Glebe Land to Working-Class Heartland:
    The Bishopsgate Street Neighbourhood   65
From Fields to Streets: Farm Street, Hockley   70
Garrisons and Artillery: Garrison Lane   75
A Clump of Rooks: Rookery Road, Handsworth   79
The Hills are Alive: Sparkhill   84
Upper and Lower Villages: Stechford   89
Land of the Bath Tub: West Heath   93
Lanes Lost in the Mist of Time: The Lost Streets of Brum   98

Chapter 4   **Hard Collar**

Rubber at the Fort: Dunlop   103
Precious Talents of Jewellery Men and Women: The Jewellery Quarter   108
A Grocer of Distinction: George Mason   112
Ale the Conquering Hero: Mitchell's and Butler's   116
Station to Station: Railway Workers   120
King of the Skies: Spitfires   126

Chapter 5   **Sights, Sounds and Smells of Old Brum**

Holtes on the Hill: Aston Hall   131
One from the Vaults: The BAI   135
Skid Kids: Cycle Speedway   139
Crowning Glory of Brum: The Old Crown   143
Sunk Without Trace: The River Rea   147
Settlement of Hope: The Summer Lane Settlement   151
When Tripe was Great: Tripe and Onion and Faggots and Peas   155

*To our forebears who
collared to give us
that which was denied
to them: a choice*

Chapter 1:

The Heart of Brum: The Bull Ring

The Bull Ring of Memory: The Old Bull Ring

It was a scene which had sped into his spirit when he had been but a toddler and now he was ageing, he had only to let his eyelids drop and his mind and soul were there once again in the Bull Ring of his childhood. Born when the nineteenth century was fast ebbing into history, the old Bull Ring had been more than his playground, it had been his whole life and nothing anywhere could have matched it.

In them years, the barrow boys lined Spiceal Street from the Market Hall down across Edgbaston Street into Jamaica Row, whilst on Tuesdays, Thursdays and Saturdays, from six in the morning the sellers of plants, shrubs, fowl, eggs and rabbits used to set up their stalls. He and so many other kids got such a thrill from running between the wooden trestles over which tarpaulin had been pulled across uprights, from minding out for the baskets from which the flower sellers hawked their wares, and from bobbing and weaving betwixt and between the flat hand carts. But the best fun of all was harking at the banter between the more street-wise, raucous city traders and the softer-voiced and calmer farm folk.

From an early age, he'd learnt how the Bull Ring could be not only a place of adventure but also a good spot to earn a copper here and a copper there by making himself useful through running errands, fetching this and carrying that. It came in handy what he earned, for with it he could buy a rabbit for his mom's stewpot or else a chicken – after bartering with the bloke who kept the fowl in a cage made of wood and wire netting close to Nelson's Statue.

So powerful was the tug of the Bull Ring that during the long school holidays of the summer he seemed to spend every hour of the day in that great triangular space which had Saint Martin's Church as its base and the lower reaches of High Street as its tip. Mind you, even when he had to go to school he'd be at the Bull Ring first thing in the morning, just about racing to Rea Street in time to get his mark. And once the bell had been rung for the end of the day, he and his pals would be shooting up to what for them was the centre of the world – Brummagem's Bull Ring.

And it wornt just in the spring and the summer that you could find him there, for even though in the winter the weather might be parky and misly there was something special about the Bull Ring in the dark nights. For then the stalls would be lit up by naphtha flares and there would be a hazy yet magical glow all around. Sadly, there were no naphtha flares today in the Bull Ring, nor youngsters running about doing this and that – but in his mind's eye there were still and always would be.

This wonderful depiction of the Bull Ring in the 1820s is one of the most famous paintings of nineteenth-century Birmingham. Its power lies not only in the magnificent way in which the artist has captured the vitality of both the Bull Ring and its people but also in its timelessness. Although showing the Bull Ring a decade after the Battle of Waterloo, this painting would reach out to anyone who recalled the Bull Ring of the 1890s, the 1920s and the 1950s. It is the Bull Ring of memory, the Bull Ring which is etched deep into the consciousness of Brummies who can recall the time before high-rise buildings and wide ring roads dominated the landscape of Birmingham.

*The painting was done by David Cox, one of the greatest of all English artists, who was bred and born in Brum and was the son of a whitesmith. It was painted from a drawing commissioned for a book, **The Graphic Illustrations of Warwickshire**, and came about after Cox had done a preliminary drawing and then another in sepia. Afterwards the drawing was engraved by a friend of Cox's, William Radclyffe – a man highly skilled in that craft which was one of the gifts to the world of art from the metal workers of Birmingham. Cox's painting is in Birmingham Museum and Art Gallery.*

Looking up the Bull Ring and Spiceal Street to High Street, Birmingham on a market morning. The photograph has been taken from Saint Martin's Church, seemingly some time in the late 1890s or early 1900s. On the right, the Central Hotel is on the corner with Park Street and it is from here that the Bull Ring as a street actually started. It carried on for a short stretch to Moor Street, which is indicated by the space between the two shops with canopies up from the Royal Coronation Waxworks. At Moor Street, the road then became High Street Birmingham. Across the way, on the left, the old Fish Market stands on the corner of Spiceal Street and Bell Street. The building across from it is the old Market Hall which signified the beginning of High Street on its west side. This photograph makes plain just how the redevelopments of the 1960s cut off the markets from the city centre by overlaying this area with the concrete collar of the Inner Ring Road. This dual carriageway swept across the line of Moor Street and Bell Street and the site of the Market Hall became part of Manzoni Gardens.

Selling live fowl in the Bull Ring in late August 1947. During the inter-war years, a shopper would often choose a bird from amongst the live chickens and taking no notice of those about him, the trader would wring the neck of the chicken to kill it and with swiftness he would rough pluck its feathers. Other shoppers preferred to buy the bird live, tuck it under their arms and take it home to kill themselves – or else they might keep it in the back yard or garden where it would be fed on boiled potato peelings and such like and would provide the family with eggs.

June Lowe, nee Bidmead, now lives in Ludlow and my **Evening Mail** articles on the Bull Ring 'evoked many memories of my childhood in the 1930s when our Saturday night treat was a trip on the Handsworth tram from the top of Villa Road to Snow Hill. We walked through the Great Western Arcade to the Bull Ring and watched the toyshop's Hornby trains, and sometimes Father Xmas was on the bridge, and there was a shop on the left, which made a kind of toffee in a machine in the window.' Just beyond was a jeweller's, 'with lumps of amethyst and beautiful little blue pictures made from butterfly wings on boxes and brush sets'.

However, what June enjoyed the most was stroking the young and not so young animals in and about the Market Hall. There was 'the African Grey Parrot, for instance, on his perch outside a shop (I think that was in Bell Street) who regularly pecked my fingers before I got dragged away. I was also quickly whisked away from the puppy cages in the market because I wanted to buy them and take them home.'

One other memory remains strong, that of the pavement artist in Worcester Street, 'down the Market Hall steps, at the back entrance, almost opposite a very good seedsman and bulb merchant named Morris. I was always given a penny to put in the artist's little black (velvet?) bag "guarded" by a large black dog, who I used to stroke. Many times since I have tried to find out the dog's breed, but nobody remembers!'

Each a Saturday when he was a schoolboy in the 1930s , Mr D. A. Elliott, used to get the 84 or 90 tram to Albert Street or Fazeley Street and then walk along to the Bull Ring, going between 'the barrows and the naphtha flares. I have memories of an electric sign on one of the buildings at the top of the hill facing down the Bull Ring (I think it was part of the Co-op known as the Louvre) in the shape of a railway locomotive. This was, of course, before the days of neon signs, and was made up of separate bulbs which were lit up in succession and gave the illusion that the wheels were revolving and smoke was coming out of the chimney. The sign itself is very vivid in my memory, but I have never found anyone else who remembers it.'

The Street of Barrow Boys: Spiceal Street

A short run it may have been, yet Spiceal Street was one of the oldest thoroughfares in Birmingham. Running downhill from the old Market Hall and Bell Street it went alongside St. Martin's in the Bull Ring and into Edgbaston Street. Originally it was called Mercer Street because it was the stretch where the textile merchants of the town had gathered. These mercers had been prominent from the emergence of Birmingham as a market place, and in 1232 one of them was noted in an early document relating to our history. With four weavers, a smith, a tailor and a purveyor, he was party to an agreement with William de Bermingham, lord of the manor. In return for each paying the great sum of £10 in cash and 2s a year they were exempted from helping at the lord's annual haymaking.

A document dating seven years later also mentioned a mercer, and in the following decade, Birmingham established itself not only as a leading market town but also as a prominent centre of cloth production. In these circumstances, mercers were likely to thrive and this interpretation seems to be substantiated by the Lay Subsidy returns of 1525. They indicated that 1576 people in Birmingham were liable to pay tax. However, 91 per cent of this total possessed only half of the wealth of the town. The other half was owned by just 9 per cent, or fourteen, of the taxpayers. Amongst this select band of wealthy Brummies were a mercer and a mercer's widow. The ongoing significance of mercers was emphasised by a Survey of Birmingham carried out in 1553, by which time a street named after them seems to have appeared.

One of the mercers of this period was John Shelton, one of the first trustees of King Edward's School. His descendants married into county families and became members of the landed gentry with lands in West Bromwich and Wednesbury. Amongst the Sheltons was Sir Richard, who was born and baptised in Birmingham in 1579 and who became Solicitor General to Charles I.

Like Digbeth, the Bull Ring and Edgbaston Street, Mercer Street became a cramped road, tightly packed with narrow buildings perhaps just 15 feet wide. An expert on early Birmingham, Joseph Hill, conjectured that they would have been 'picturesque, overhanging and painted, gabled, half-timbered erections of the Tudor period'. Still, the gutters would have been dirty; rubbish heaps – miskins – would have been plentiful, the streets would have been laid with large stones set in gravel and the badly-kept footpaths would have been bound up with staves and timber.

By the early 1700s, Mercer Street was also known as Spicer Street and at the end of that century it had become Spiceal Street. According to William Hutton, Birmingham's first historian, this was because mercers dealt in grocery and spices and so Spiceal was a corruption of Spicer. Because mercers were not grocers it is difficult to accept this explanation, and indeed by Hutton's time Spiceal Street was characterised by butcher's stalls and not sellers of spice. Whatever the origins of its name, Spiceal Street was marked out at its top end by the 'Dog Inn', above which was the land owned by the Cowper family – after whom is named Cowper Street in Summer Lane, and upon which the fish market would be built.

This is a magnificent shot of Spiceal Street on a quiet market day, or at a quiet time of a market day. There is so much to grab hold of. The tobacconist's of C. S. Hawkesford and Son is in the front of the old Fish Market and is the first retailer in Spiceal Street at the corner with Bell Street. Next door is the well-known premises of Wheatlands Limited, house furnishers and then comes the great Woolworth's store which dominated Spiceal Street. Below that is a large building covered with scaffolding and which housed Smart's the butcher's as well as a variety of businesses from solicitors and sugar importers to safe makers and industrial painting contractors. The last retailer in Spiceal Street, on the corner with Edgbaston Street, was W. B. S. Blindells Ltd, the boot and shoe dealers.

But, of course, the shopkeepers were only part of the attraction of Spiceal Street for it was here that stood the market traders who brought both the street itself and the Bull Ring fully into live. Loud, colourful and witty, the street traders placed their handcarts in a line down the hill and across the junction of Saint Martin's Lane and Edgbaston Street and into Jamaica Row. On the left and on the corner of Saint Martin's Lane and Jamaica Row can be seen the imposing structure of the Saint Martin's Hotel. By contrast to the variety and activity on the west side of Spiceal Street, its east side was taken up by one building – that of Saint Martin's Church.

For all the increased overcrowding locally there were still houses with gardens in Spiceal Street, as was indicated by an advertisement for the sale of property in 1798. It offered 'two commodious dwelling houses with separate court in front, a considerable range of shops, a large garden, a stable and other out offices and conveniences'; and it was declared that 'the centrical Site of the Premises in the Town, may render them eligible to a Merchant, Factor, or Manufacturer, or to a Broker, Pawnbroker.'

In later years, many people came to forget the name of Spiceal Street but it remained a crucial road at the heart of Brum. Indeed, the well-remembered Woolworth's in the Bull Ring was actually in Spiceal Street – as was Wheatland's the house furnishers, Smart's the pork butchers and Hipkins the safe makers.

Sadly, the Council did away with the term Spiceal Street as part of its transformation of the Bull Ring area in the late 1950s and early 1960s. Yet, if the name is gone, the street itself still runs downhill from where the underpass used to be below the Inner Ring Road, in front of the now demolished 1960s Market Hall and alongside Saint Martin's and into Edgbaston Street.

The redevelopments of the mid-twentieth century were not the first to have affected Spiceal Street. By the close of the 1700s, the markets of Brum were scattered all over the town: corn and vegetables were sold in the Bull Ring; meat was bought in the Shambles just above Saint Martin's; flowers and shrubs were hawked at the end of Phillips Street (which disappeared under the Inner Ring Road); cattle was traded in Dale End; pigs, horses and sheep were bought in the Swine Market at the bottom of New Street; and fruit, fowl and butter were purchased by the Old Cross. Within a few years, a hay and straw market was set up in Ann Street (now Colmore Row), and a fish market was begun in Dale End.

This spreading out of the markets led to severe congestion and accidents on market and other days. Such overcrowding was made worse by the clutter of buildings which hemmed in Saint Martin's. In 1806 the Street Commissioners, an unelected body of leading citizens which was Brum's only form of local government, acted to solve these problems. The houses on the east side of Spiceal Street and the west side of the Bull Ring were pulled down.

This clearance led to the disappearance of a number of tiny streets such as The Shambles and Cock Street. This was that stretch of the modern Digbeth between Park Street and Allison Street which also was called Well Street and Well Yard, indicating the plentiful water supply locally. Another street to be lost was Corn Cheaping, which had run alongside Saint Martin's from Park Street to Moor Street. The Old English word ceping or cieping meant a market and in Birmingham it was used to indicate where the sellers of corn gathered. This name was of great age and is noted in a deed from 1685.

The action of the street commissioners allowed the forming of that great triangular space of land which had Saint Martin's as its base and the bottom of High Street as its top point and which is the Bull Ring recalled so affectionately by many Brummies. Such an opening up led to the injunction that no stalls should be set up above Phillips Street. Market traders were to gather now in the Bull Ring which had been at the heart of the Medieval town and where there was ample room 'for every purpose of that kind'.

Another old street was a continuation downhill of Spiceal Street. This was Jamaica Row. By the publication of Thomas Hanson's Map of Birmingham in 1778, there was a Black Boy Yard running downhill from the junction of Edgbaston Street and Saint Martin's Lane. It took its name from an inn on the corner of the two roads – the 'Black Boy' which referred to the dark looks of Charles II. Formerly, the 'Black Boy' had been the 'Woolpack'. The yard became part of Jamaica Row, which thus swept down from Spiceal Street, past the old manor house and into Moat Lane. Jamaica Row was thrust from the face of Brum by the changes wrought after the Second World War.

Would it not be fitting that Spiceal Street should be reinstated in the forthcoming redevelopment of the Bull Ring as it is one of the half dozen streets which link us with our roots in the Middle Ages – and perhaps Jamaica Row, Corn Cheaping, Cock Street, and The Shambles should also be brought back to life.

A smashing photo of Spiceal Street on a bustling market day in the Bull Ring in 1958. The shoppers in the foreground are in front of the old Market Hall – and notice the copper on the right. Below the balloon seller and the chap flogging what seem to be hoop-las are what look like two Romany women offering lucky heather to anyone who wants to buy it. They are standing opposite Bell Street and you can see clearly the pillars of the old Fish Market denoting the beginning of Spiceal Street. It is a wonderful scene, with shoppers and traders flowing down past Woolworth's and into Jamaica Row.

*Norman Haddon now lives in West Sussex. His sister. Sylvia O'Brien, sent him my **Evening Mail** articles on the Bull Ring which 'brought tears to my eyes and a lump to my throat'. Now 75 years old, Norman recalls that his father* was employed by the City of Birmingham Salvage Department at the Montague Street depot. He was George William Haddon and his job was go collect all the rubbish and refuse from all of the markets 'from the Market Hall, down to the Meat Market abattoir, including the Fish Market in Bell Street, the Green Market (as we called it) and the Rag Market etc., – all in his little electricity lorry'.

From when he was about six years old, Norman's mom would take him on a Saturday morning to the Bull Ring where she got all her fruits and vegetables: 'we would then meet Dad in which ever market he was working, and whilst Mother went home on the 31A/32 bus, I would stay with dad for the remainder of the working day'. When war came, Norman's Dad immediately joined the Home Guard, and as an ex-serviceman he became a corporal in the Montague Street Company of the 29th Warwickshire Battalion. Sadly, 'a few months later tragedy overtook our family when on the night of Tuesday/Wednesday 16th October 1940 the Germans dropped a mine directly on the works, destroying it and 15 men's lives with it'. Most of the men who were killed were night staff, but six of them were members of the Home Guard. Amongst them was George William Haddon. His name is recorded and remembered in Saint Martin's Church as well as in the Hall of Memory. Poignantly, Norman explains, 'so you see, Carl, to us the Bull Ring is sacred and they destroyed it'.

Maud Mason also wrote to me with 'eyes blurred with tears'. She is now living in Ohio in the USA and the articles were sent to her by her sister Lily George. When the two of them were little and living in Balsall Heath Road, 'my brothers used to walk us up to the Bull Ring – starting from the bottom of it we'd mooch to the Fruit Market and the Rag Market, some days stopping there to listen to the sales pitch of the men who sold china in baskets. I was always fond of beautiful china cups and saucers which I never did have until a relative gave me as a gift some Royal Albert Country Roses! When we came in 1959 to this country I carried them away with me.'

On those visits to the Bull Ring, Maud and her brothers and sisters would eventually work their way to the top of the Bull Ring and go into the Market Hall to look at the wondrous clock. Mrs H. Everitt is another person who recalls the clock with affection. Now 78 years old, 'I well remember my father taking me to town to watch the clock. It was so fascinating. It was so sad to see it go, also the Market Hall where I went and bought all my curtain material so I could make my own curtains when I was married in 1941'. Like many other folk who have written to me, Mrs Everitt agrees with me that we should have a new clock with figures from Birmingham's history.

*For many years, Rick Green took superb photos of Brum. This one shows the way the markets'
traffic used to block up Jamaica Row. Amidst the cars and vans, men are also shifting produce on
hand carts and trolleys. On the right is the 'Smithfield Arms' pub, and out of shot to its right was
the original Smithfield Garage. The rest of the street was filled with fruit merchants and brokers,
corn merchants, potato salesman, meat salesmen and seedsmen as well as with folk not directly
connected with the markets – such as tailors, tobacconists and paper merchants. Jamaica Row also
boasted a manufacturer of refrigerators, three banks, a Salvation Army Hostel for Working Men,
Albert Daniel's restaurant and a branch of Oswald Bailey's Army and Navy Stores.*

*Rick Green told me that these external premises of the markets were known as 'the Fringe', and
he points out that walking up from the Bromsgrove Street end of Jamaica Row is a policeman,
obviously about to try and sort out the blockage. The photograph itself was taken by Rick as he lay
along a parapet with a light four foot plank under his left elbow. His camera was screwed down on
a mount at the outer end and a piece of string worked the shutter.*

The Thrill of Market Day

It was a rumbustious yet invigorating day was market day, although now and then the crowds and their roistering ways did make you a bit nervy. Sometimes you got yourself that het up with all the milling about and rushing to and fro that you thought you'd stay close to home on a Thursday, but then the collywobbles'd start racing round your tummy and you'd get a kind of shiver that would make you shift and lift your shoulders and you knew that the markets were calling.

Off you set, that summer's day in the early 1780s, thinking you wouldn't plunge straightaway into the hustle and bustle down by the Bull Ring. No, instead you'd gradually get used to the noise and fast movement by heading first for Dale End where Brum's few fishmongers were clustered. Mind you their pitch was only a small space of relative quiet, for nearby the air was rent by the bellowing of cows and the calls of farmers in the cattle market.

Dodging aside from a mass of hooves, bobbing out of the way of a medley of turning heads, and ducking out of the road from a mess of splayed arms, she came to the Welsh Cross, close to the junction with Bull Street. What a haven of slower movements and quieter chatter where you could buy your cheese from this monger and that monger. Then the crowds began to flow again more powerfully as she was almost dragged along High Street towards the junction with the bottom end of New Street, whence came a right cacophony – the shouts of men, the snorts of pigs, the bleating of sheep and the whinnying of horses.

She was never attracted to that part of the market, but even if she had been she would have had a job and a half to have turned uphill, for the strong flow of the crowd was downwards. And down she went, coming round the broad bend which indicated the end of the upper section of High Street and the start of the lower part of that thoroughfare.

Almost at the bottom of High Street, at the end of Phillips Street where the Market Hall would be built early in the next century, there were sellers of flowers and shrubs. Just across the way was the Old Cross – well it was called a cross but it was really a four-sided building. Each side had two arches and open entrances and traders gathered inside when the weather was bad. Above was a room surmounted by a clock and a little cupola with a weather vane above it. The Welsh Cross was a similar structure, and its upper room often had been used as a military guardhouse.

Behind the Old Cross were two lines of buildings which filled the area which was later a clear space around Nelson's Statue. The one row of houses and shops was the east side of Spiceal Street and the other was the west side of the Bull Ring. These structures hemmed in Saint Martin's and almost hid it from view, bar for its tower. The cluttered look was made even more cramped by the stalls and baskets of folk hawking fruit and vegetables and flogging earthenware all down the Bull Ring towards Park Street, and also by the standings of more shrub and flower sellers at the junction with Moor Street. If they weren't enough, there was trestle after trestle from which was sold corn.

This is a really evocative shot of the Bull Ring on a market day in the late 1800s. These women who are selling plants and shrubs have set up their stalls in the best pitches possible, in front of the magnificent columns of the old Market Hall. Notice the hats that are worn by these female traders and the billycocks sported by most of the men. At this time, the billycock – bowler hat – was the headgear of the working man. The pub on the left and behind the street lamp is the 'Board Vaults'. It is on the corner of High Street and Phillips Street. On the opposite corner is the superb old Market Hall and can you see the rugs hanging up outside Paul Taylor's carpet warehouse. This store remained on site until the Market Hall was demolished. The equivalent retail space on the left-hand side of the building was occupied by the dining rooms of the celebrated Mrs Hannah Mountford.

Today Birmingham is renowned as one of the great manufacturing cities of the world and is gaining a growing reputation for its role as a centre for the leisure and convention and conference industries. But none should forget that in the first instance it was the markets which made Brum. In the later Anglo-Saxon age and during the century following the Norman Conquest, Birmingham was an insignificant manor with a very small population. That situation was transformed after 1166 when Peter de Bermingham gained the right to hold a weekly market.

As lord of a manor which was worth little, he could see the possibilities of making money from charging a toll on market traders and from renting plots of land to people who would be attracted to live and set up business close to a market. Although there is no firm evidence stating exactly where the market was held, it is almost certain that it was in the vicinity of the modern Bull Ring and close to Saint Martin's Church.

Peter and his descendants had their manor house nearby. It was knocked down in the early nineteenth century and today the site is occupied by the wholesale markets. The manor house was encircled by a moat, hence Moat Lane and the now-disappeared Moat Row – which used to run from Bromsgrove Street to the bottom of Bradford Street.

Although it was clamorous and roisterous, this was her favourite part of the markets – in spite of her nerviness. It seemed as if the whole world had come to Brum and the Bull Ring. Indeed it had – her world at least. Here she would try and find a spot by a building where she could stand and take it all in and rarely would she move away to venture down Spiceal Street – for there were the sights, sounds and smells which really did scare her. For in Spiceal Street were the butchers' stalls, where animals were killed and – well she didn't like to think about it. There she stood in the packed Bull Ring, sucking the scene into her soul, until night had drawn in and it was time to hurry home.

An unusual view of the Bull Ring in what would appear to be the 1930s. The photographer has taken his picture from below the tarpaulin protecting one of the stalls. Interestingly he is not facing Spiceal Street and the landmarks of Woolworth's, the old Fish Market and the old Market Hall, instead he is looking across more stalls towards the lower end of High Street, just before the junction with Moor Street and the beginnings of the road called the Bull Ring. You can easily identify the noted army and navy store of Oswald Bailey. In the mid-1950s, this was next door to Woodleys, the house furnishers which adjoined the Bull Ring Café and confectionery shop of Leo Devoti – a member of a famed Italian Brummie family. Then came Pimm's the bird and animal dealers, Lush's the upholsterers, Burton Montague the tailor's and the Times Furnishing Building. This last structure now begins High Street and is occupied by Waterstone's. Once again. a powerful photograph emphasises how the post-war redevelopment of Birmingham and in particular the Inner Ring Road obliterated the ancient street patterns of our city. Finally, you can just notice the base of Nelson's Statue on the far left of the shot, just below the end of tarpaulin.

Another unusual view of the Bull Ring, this time taken in the late 1950s. The photographer must be standing on the corner of Moor Street, given the bend in the white lines in the middle of the horse road. He is looking across to Nelson's Statue at a time when the post-war redevelopment has already claimed the old Fish Market. This has disappeared and would have filled in the space between Wheatland's Furnishers and Bell Street. Because the Fish Market has gone, you can see down Bell Street and appreciate the architectural glory of the old Market Hall. If you then cast your eyes at the stately entrance to the building, then clear sky is obvious. Of course, the roof of the Market Hall was destroyed during the Second World War.

Beryl Chant had an auntie who used to work in Mark's and Spencer's Bazaar in the Market Hall at the start of the twentieth century. The shop used to sell all sorts of haberdashery and 'she told me how they used to have to go down into the cellar to get water etc. and how the rats were scurrying around her feet. They used to work long hours, it was 11 p.m. on Saturday nights when they finished. She used to walk home some nights to save the tram fare to buy some ribbon or a yard of lace to trim a blouse up for Sunday. After a while she was moved to the warehouse, which I believe was where Mark's and Spencer's is today. She had to leave when she got married in the First World War as they didn't employ married women at the time.' In later years, Beryl's aunt was delighted to be fetched into Mark's and Spencer's for tea. She was picked up in a taxi and was given a hamper and a bouquet, and her photo was put in the firm's newsletter.

A Wondrous Building: The Old Market Hall

It was the best spot anywhere, standing on the steps of the Market Hall and looking down at the whirling crowds and harking at the hubbub in the Bull Ring below. Mind you, because of the force of the folk going to and fro it was some feat to be able to stay still on one of these nine steps which went up from Spiceal Street and into the great building.

But that was part of the fun, striving to keep your feet planted in one spot whilst you let your body sway backwards and forwards with the rhythm of the shoppers – and all the while you shifted your head and stretched your neck so that you could still look at what was going on. No-one took any cotter of you and that was a bit strange for you were in one of the busiest places – if not the busiest place – in Brum. Hundreds upon hundreds of people passed you and you were at the centre of everything in the city – yet to everyone who passed by, you were another face, another shopper, another person waiting to meet someone.

Now and then there was a short respite in the numbers going hither and thither and that was the time you liked the best, for now you could allow yourself to move back a little and strain your muscles to look up at the magnificent Market Hall. And magnificent it was. Two massive, Doric columns supported the wide and high entrance across which metal gates were pulled at closing time. From each of the columns there struck out ornate pieces of ironwork from which hung lamps, and on either side was a really big window which was oval in shape. Made up of lots of small panes of glass, it would not have looked out of place in a big bank or a mighty cathedral.

After looking in wonder at the front of the building, you'd invariably decide to join the fast current of shoppers heading into the Market Hall. You knew all the awesome figures to do with it. The building was 365 feet long, 180 feet wide and 60 feet high and it was pierced by a central hall. It was thrilling to see such a variety of things to buy. There were the fishmongers, distinguished by their white coats and bluff expressions, standing behind stalls above which hung game and on which were laid out fish – the sight of which could take you to any part of the world you wanted.

Over there, were the women who stood in front of a colourful blaze of flowers arranged in upright boxes and pots, whilst nearby apples, pears and much more were piled high on sloping stands attended by ruddy-faced fruiterers. Then there were a tantalising array of fancy good traders, but perhaps the most compelling sellers were those who offered pets to the public. There were large-eyed puppies, softly-furred kittens, scampering guinea pigs, shy rabbits and pigeons desperate for the freedom of the sky.

Birmingham's Market Hall a magical world for the folk of Brum. Why did they have to knock it down?

A wonderful shot of the old Market Hall in 1935 when it was lit up as a rehearsal for the proper lighting up which would take place as part of the Pageant of Birmingham. This celebrated Birmingham's centenary as an incorporated borough, whereby an elected council was given powers by an act of Parliament to run the city. On the right of the Market Hall, and on the corner of Phillips Street, is Paul Taylor's warehouse where you could buy bedding, carpets and lino; to the left, and on the corner of Bell Street, the words 'Fish Stores' are illuminated. These premises had been Mountford's dining rooms and later were occupied by the poultry business of Henry Normansell. Following the consolidation of most of Birmingham's markets in the Bull Ring area after 1806, the Street Commissioners (the body which ran Birmingham then) realised that a covered market-place was needed to stand alongside the outdoor markets. The first step was to buy the market rights from the lord of the manor, and in 1824 Christopher Musgrove sold his interest for £12,500. Four years later, an act of Parliament gave the Street Commissioners the power to purchase properties between Bell Street and Phillips Street.

By 1832, all of the properties needed had been bought – bar for two whose owners held out for too high a price. To overcome this difficulty, it was decided to erect two houses 'with handsome shop fronts' on either side of the front of the Market Hall. The leases for these were sold at an auction to raise the funds which were required to pay the sums demanded by the last two property owners. Later these premises were occupied by Paul Taylor and Henry Normansell.

The Market Hall itself was built by Dewsbury and Walthews and opened on February 12, 1835. Including the cost of acquiring both the site and the properties and of construction, the total outlay on the scheme was £44,800. It was 365 feet in length, 180 feet wide and 60 feet high. With such dimensions, it dominated the landscape at the bottom of the High Street, stretching as it did all the way to Worcester Street and virtually filling the whole of the space between Bell Street and Phillips Street.

But it wasn't only the size of the Market Hall which drew the breath of onlookers and had folk shaking their heads in amazement. This building wasn't just large, it was also grand. It had two main entrances in High Street and Worcester Street, and impressively both were flanked by two mighty Doric columns. Behind them were massive archways and above them were elegant porticoes. Large yet graceful, the structure looked as if it had been transplanted from ancient Athens into the midst of industrial Brum. The vast majority of Brummies in the 1830s had seen nothing like it, for no other building in Birmingham shouted out so loud a bond between one of the world's greatest manufacturing towns and the greatest city state of Classical Greece. Of course, within a few years local folk would get used to that look, what with the Town Hall and the hotel at Curzon Street Railway Station. But for now, that kind of structure was fresh, inspiring and breathtaking.

If anything, it was even more so after the gloaming had faded into evening. For then the interior of the Market Hall was lighted with gas for the benefit of traders and shoppers alike. In all, the building boasted 600 odd stalls 'fitted up for the sale of fruit, game and poultry, fish, butcher's meat, fancy articles, live pets, etc.' For the next 100 years and more, traders continued to sell the same goods and Brummies carried on flocking to the Market Hall. Indeed, after the war the Market Hall, still with no roof, was re-opened and once again it drew in Brummies. What a pity it was not restored to its full splendour. Instead in 1963 it was knocked down after the new Bull Ring Centre Market Hall was opened.

Mrs N. Usher has a connection with the bomb which blew the roof off the Market Hall. Her brother-in-law, Sid Wainwright, was the day watchman 'and when he went to work early on the day it was bombed he had a stroke and didn't work again'. Mrs Usher adds that within the Market Hall there was a piano where 'someone used to play any pieces you wanted and then late on Saturdays they would sell off things cheaply which my mother would buy as we were not very well off'.

On one memorable occasion there was a huge crowd in the Bull Ring. The reason the people had gathered was to hear Ramsay Macdonald, the leader of the Labour Party. And Albert and Elsie recall the open air Gospel Meetings which were held at the bottom of the Bull Ring about 1935. Organised by some members of Gospel Halls, they took place at 8 o'clock on a Saturday night and at about 9 o'clock on a Sunday evening. Albert and Elsie actually met at one of these meetings.

An unusual photo of the rear entrance of the old Market Hall in Worcester Street in 1954. The cars on the right are in Bell Street, on the nearest corner of which stood the 'Board Vaults' pub. On the left the workman is drilling at the junction with Station Street and behind him and the car can be picked out an entrance to Birmingham New Street Station. Just out of shot and to the left of the workman would have been Old Meeting Street. The arches of the old Market Hall have been bricked up and the lack of roof to the structure is apparent. This roof had been lost as a result of an air raid by the Luftwaffe August 25, 1940. In fact, this was the first major night attack by German bombers on Britain during the Second World War. Birmingham's city centre was pounded by 50 enemy aircraft and incendiaries as well as a high explosive bomb hit Birmingham's Market Hall. Fortunately, the raid happened on a Sunday when the building was empty bar for its night-watchman, Mr V. Leverington. With ease he could have fled from the flames and made for safety. He did not do so, for he was concerned about all the animals which were kept for sale in the Market Hall.

Bravely, Mr Leverington 'unlocked the cages containing live creatures and released the stock, which made for the swing doors and so into the street'. Only then did the valiant night-watchman head for shelter. For his courage he was awarded the R.S.P.C.A. silver medal. A few days after the attack, the Market Hall was described as a shell with just its walls standing. Inside was a mass of rubble, charred beams, pieces of iron, bricks and a few utensils. All that remained intact were the iron frames of the stalls. One of them had the name plaque 'Albert Pope' and on it 'two small Union Jacks had been bravely stuck in the wreckage'. Further along, the firm of Yates had chalked the notice of their new address alongside the words, 'Burnt but not broke'.

Vic Letherington was Pam Hunt's grandfather and 'my grandmother always blamed this incident on his death a few years later because the iron gate fell onto him after he had released the animals, causing him much pain and suffering'. Despite the sadness associated with that horrible night, Pam has added an amusing story: 'as you said Vic went into the market to release the animals, but one tiny puppy would not leave his side and kept following him back into the market. So Vic popped him into his overcoat pocket and eventually took him home to his wife and three children. "Little Ruff" as he was called turned into a "Big Ruff", an Irish wolf hound.'

Taken in the late 1930s, this inside view of the old Market Hall highlights the famous and much-loved clock on the left of the picture. This fascinating feature which appealed to both youngsters and their moms and dads was put in the building in 1936. Placed on a veranda, it was a beautiful clock which boasted three bells, the largest of which weighed three hundredweight. Upon the hour and the half hour, these bells were struck by one of four solid oak figures – three of which were medieval knights and one of which was a damsel.

Each of the two middle figures was 7 feet 6 inches in height, whilst each of the two outer figures was six feet high. All of them were made of solid oak. Above the figures was the dial. Measuring five feet across and having an area of fifteen square feet, it weighed fifteen hundred weight and boasted a pendulum of two hundredweight, a main wheel and barrel and a bed of three hundredweight.

Constructed in 1883 by Messrs Potts and Son of Leeds, originally the spectacular clock was placed in the Imperial Arcade in Dale End in 1883. However, the clock stopped ticking and striking after twenty years. Then in the mid-1930s 'Our Percy' Shurmer, the chairman of the council's Markets' Committee, had the clock repaired and brought to the Market Hall. It was unveiled by the Lord Mayor, Alderman J. S. Grey, on March 13, 1936 and immediately it became the biggest attraction in the markets, especially on a Saturday when crowds would gather below the clock to see its figures strike its bells.

Sadly, the clock was destroyed by the fire which swept through the Market Hall following the German air raid of 25 August 1940. Only one of the bells survived, whilst all of the figures were burned to ashes. A month after the loss of the clock, Percy Shurmer declared that after the war, the British Government should confiscate a similar clock from Munich. That did not happen, but would it not be a wonderful thing if in the new Bull Ring there would be a new and grand clock with figures striking bells? And could not those figures represent the people of the Bull Ring, perhaps a woman flower seller, an Italian ice cream seller, a 'Spatch and Mail vendor and a speaker such as Holy Joe or Ernie McCulloch?

Custodian of the Soul of Brum: Saint Martin's

Saint Martin's Church and the Bull Ring markets. The two are bonded so deeply that none could ever break the connection between them. Both emerged at the dawning of Brum's rise to fame as a manufacturing centre, and both continue to thrive as Birmingham sets out to establish itself as a city noted for its leisure and convention industries.

Saint Martin's and the Bull Ring markets. The two are the only constants in a city renowned for its speedy grasping of change, its perpetual search for innovation, and its thirst for thrusting itself forward and reaching out for the future. Through all the transformations of our town, the market folk and the clergy of Saint Martin's have been the custodians of the soul of Brum.

Some people feel that there may have been a small church in the manor of Birmingham during the time of the Anglo Saxons, but there is little hard evidence to support this case. What we do know is that about 1250 – less than 100 years after the markets first started – an older church was replaced by a more expensive and grander building.

It was named after Saint Martin, a cavalryman in the Roman army who became a Christian after he had helped an almost naked beggar who lay shivering in the cold on the roadside in Amiens in Gaul – now France. Touched by the man's troubles, Saint Martin took his sword, cut his cloak in half and gave one part to the trembling pauper. That night the kindly soldier dreamed that his actions were told by Jesus to the angels. Soon after Saint Martin was baptised and left the army to become ordained. There are many stories as to his courage and faithfulness and later he became Bishop of Tours.

Just as Saint Martin shared his cloak, so too has the church named after him shared itself with the people of Birmingham and within its walls it holds three important tombs from the early history of our city. Each of them has representations of members of the de Bermingham family – lords of the manor of Brum from at least 1135 until 1536.

One of the effigies is in the style of the late thirteenth or early fourteenth century and is that of a Sir William – although it is difficult to state who it is in particular for in that period Birmingham had four lords of that name. Whatever the case, it has been claimed that this representation is the oldest surviving work of art in Birmingham. The second de Bermingham tomb in stone is that of Sir Fulk, one of the most powerful members of his family. He was a prominent warrior in the wars against the French and in 1346 fought at the Battle of Crécy when the English bowmen destroyed a larger French force. Ten years later, it is also likely that he was present at another great victory at Poitiers. The third effigy is in alabaster and is that of Fulk's son, Sir John, who is shown in armour.

Unfortunately, substantial building work on Saint Martin's in the eighteenth century meant that many other ancient monuments were destroyed. Amongst the few other surviving features from the past are a wooden memorial erected to William Colmore – one of the family after which Colmore Row and Great Colmore Street were

It's a quarter past one on a market day in the 1800s and overlooking this atmospheric scene is Saint Martin's in the Bull Ring. The traders have been set up for hours, shoppers are mooching about – and if they fancy they can buy a delicious ice cream from the Italian ice-cream seller placed handily with his cart between two of the lampposts guarding Nelson's Statue. Once again, notice how many of the traders are women. By contrast most of the hawkers with their hand carts who lined Spiceal Street and Jamaica Row were men.

A most moving photograph of Norman and Renee Smith at the altar of Saint Martin's Church at their wedding on April 17, 1941. This was the first wedding to take place in our parish church after the destruction wrought by the German air raid of April 9 and 10. Sixty years later, on their diamond wedding anniversary, their blessing celebrations fittingly took place at Saint Ma rtin's. Thanks to their daughter, Christine Scott.

It was a miracle that Saint Martin's survived that terrible air raid which began at 9.35 on the night of April 9 and went on into the early hours of the next morning. Birmingham was blasted by two hundred bombers which dropped 170 sets of incendiaries and 650 high explosive bombs, one of which fell on the approach way to the west door of the church.

The high explosive made a crater amidst the graves, blew away pinnacles, tore holes in the masonry and stonework, and blasted the great oak framework the door itself from its base – and yet somehow a statue of Saint Martin stood untouched in a niche on the western facade. Inside the place of worship, pews had been battered, stained glass had been shattered, oak beams had been wrenched from their positions and debris had been scattered everywhere.

Amidst this scene of destruction, there was a remarkable survival. In its north and south transepts, Saint Martin's possessed windows designed by that internationally-acclaimed Birmingham artist, Edward Burne-Jones. The day before the air raid, they had been removed, packed and placed in the south porch where they lay undamaged.

Despite the devastation the rector of Saint Martin's decided to carry on with the Good Friday services the next day. With the help of his wife, the churchwardens, other clergymen, shop assistants and market traders, the worst of the rubble was cleared up so that worship could be carried on. That indomitable spirit led to the Lord Mayor of Birmingham declaring on VE Day that 'the parish church itself is a fine symbol of the triumph of freedom over tyranny for, although it suffered badly from enemy damage, it continued its fine work courageously throughout the years of the war and will, I hope, for all time hold the warm affection and devotion of the people of Birmingham whom it has served for centuries'.

named; the Chantry Chapel dedicated to the Clodeshales, the family which owned Saltley in the 1300s; and the Thorne Memorial Chapel of the Guild of the Holy Cross – out of the estates of which King Edward VI School was endowed.

The tower and spire of Saint Martin's are the oldest parts of the church itself and were restored in the mid-nineteenth century, whilst the rest of the church was taken down and rebuilt between 1872 and 1875. Although most of the church is relatively recent, Saint Martin's harks back to our beginnings and stands as it has done always – at the heart of the city.

It's five and twenty-past two on a sluggish market day in the summer some time in the 1950s. As it has done throughout our history as a major settlement, Saint Martin's and the markets provide constants in our ever-changing landscape. The railings around Nelson's Statue are on the left and next to the flower seller is a bloke flogging eggs. Just below him, some goods laid out on the ground have caught the eyes of a few passers by, and on the left of the telephone boxes a copper seems to be having a chat.

This apparently timeless scene is soon to be swept away from the face of Brum. The hoardings hide the building site which has replaced the structures which once went along the Bull Ring from the corner of Park Street and up to Moor Street and the start of High Street. In a few years, this plot would become a multi-storey car park underneath which were the 'Slowboat' Chinese restaurant and other new premises. These, too, have been knocked down in the most recent redevelopment of the Bull Ring and now Moor Street runs down into that space. On the corner of Park Street is the 'Royal George'. Although this particular structure was cleared, another pub of the same name still stands here. Alongside it and in Park Street is a building at the ground floor of which would be 'Lorenzo's Italian restaurant and above which would be a karate centre. Originally, this was the London Museum and Concert Hall which opened in 1863. Known as 'The Mucker', it was a place at which money was raised for poor children. Closed as music hall in 1900, 'The Mucker' reopened as the Bull Ring Cinema in 1912. Its days as a picture house ended in 1931.

Honoured First in Brum: Nelson's Statue

It was one of the most thrilling events in the history of Birmingham, the visit of Lord Nelson on Monday August 29, 1802. Acclaimed as one the greatest of English sea captains in the wars against the French and their allies, he had played a vital part in the defeat of the Spanish fleet off Cape Saint Vincent in 1797, as a result of which he was knighted. Soon after, he lost his right arm in battle and then in 1798, he led a daring attack on the French fleet in Aboukir Bay and gained a famous victory.

Lord Nelson arrived late in Brum, but within minutes word of his coming had flown around the town. The bells of Saint Martin's were rung and an immense crowd collected outside the hotel at which was staying 'the gallant Admiral who had so nobly fought and bled in his country's service'. The huge gathering repeatedly called for Nelson to show himself and each time he came to the window he was greeted with applauding shouts.

That night Nelson and his party were accompanied by the dignitaries of Birmingham to the Theatre Royal. Upon 'the entrance of his Lordship the band struck up "Rule Britannia" and the whole house rose and testified, by their unanimous and long continued plaudits, the gratification they experienced' at the sight of the well-loved warrior. The next day, Nelson visited some of the great manufactories of Birmingham, amongst them Henry Clay's japanning works; the button factory of W. and R. Smith; Francis Eginton's stained glass works; and the Soho Manufactory of Matthew Boulton. Wherever he went, he was accompanied by 'a very large crowd of people, repeatedly huzzaing'.

On the evening, Nelson again went to the theatre and the next morning viewed more places of manufacture before setting off for Warwick. Before he left, 'his Lordship expressed, in the strongest terms, the sense he entertained of the very respectful attention which had been shewn him, and the pleasure and satisfaction he had experienced during his stay in the town'.

Just over three years, on October 21, 1805, Nelson triumphed over the French at the Battle of Trafalgar, but according to the *Gazette*, when the word came 'never was the victorious banner so darkened and discoloured as this has been by the death of the glorious and intrepid Chief, through whose skilful arrangements, aided by congenial spirits, the conquest was achieved. This fell discord marred the general harmony of opinion. Every man smiled at the great news of the victory; but when the price was told the smile was followed by a sigh.'

In honour of Nelson, Matthew Boulton struck a fine commemorative medal of the battle at which he was killed. With the government's permission, the famed Brummagem manufacturer gave one to each person who had taken part in the action. Flag officers and commanders received copies in gold, lieutenants were given them in silver and the men were handed medals in bronze.

Landlocked as we are, the men of Brum have been conspicuous in service in the Royal Navy and on November 23, 1805, a meeting was held 'to take into consideration

This is a cracking shot of Thomas Pitt standing with his barrow to the side of Nelson's Statue and with the old Fish Market in the background. Notice the railings around the statue and the bicycle close to them. Thomas was the grandfather of Mrs V. Townsend, herself late of Irving Street, and he was the road sweeper for the Bull Ring area. Thomas is one of those people who could have been forgotten from history if it had not been for his grand-daughter. He was one of the many people who carried out jobs that were taken from granted and which were not recorded officially. Yet, Thomas and Brummies like him played vital roles in the making of our city. They should never be forgotten.

some plan for erecting a Monument, Statue, or Pillar, to the memory of the late gallant hero, Lord Nelson.' It was resolved unanimously that such a memorial should be erected on or near the site of the Old Cross – where the Inner Ring now runs across the Bull Ring.

Money poured into the fund which was set up and on June 13, 1806 the subscribers instructed Richard Westmacott to sculpt a likeness of the great hero. The people of Brum raised £2,500 to pay the sculptor and a further £500 for the pedestal, lamps and palisading. The corner posts were made of old cannon from Nelson's ship, the 'Victory'.

The scaffolding which surrounded the statue was taken down at midnight on October 24, 1809, 'and recognising Birmingham was the first place in Britain to honour the hero with a statue, the people enthusiastically assisting the workmen in removing it'. The next day, the statue itself was uncovered 'amid great rejoicing'. Westmacott himself explained his work. It was intended to perpetuate 'the greatest example of naval genius' and simplicity was the chief object. Nelson is represented in 'a reposed and dignified attitude' with his left arm reclining on an anchor draped in a sail. He appears 'in the costume of his native country, invested with the insignia of those honours by which his sovereign and distant princes distinguished him'.

Commander A. O. Watson, chairman of the Navy League in Birmingham, placing a laurel and chrysanthemum anchor beneath Nelson's Statue in Birmingham's Bull Ring, to commemorate Trafalgar Day 21 October 1954. This ceremony was carried out each year and when Nelson's Statue is placed once again in honour in the Bull Ring then we should ensure that the tradition is revived.

Lord Nelson's statue has been surrounded by scaffolding and soon it will be moved as part of the root and branch post-war redevelopment of Birmingham. Taken in September 1958, it highlights the death throes of the old Bull Ring. Soon this flower seller and her fellow traders will have been shunted from their traditional pitches and placed in unfamiliar spots.

To the right was 'the grand symbol of the naval profession' and 'Victory', 'the constant attendant upon her favourite hero, embellishes the prow'. Above the ship is a facsimile of 'the Flag Staff Truck of L'Orient, which was fished up by Sir Samuel Hood the day following the Battle of the Nile, and presented by him to Lord Nelson'.

The whole group is mounted upon a circular pedestal of statuary marble. Finally, 'to personify that affectionate regard which caused the present patriotic tribute to be raised, the town, Birmingham, is represented in a dejected attitude, murally crowned, mourning her loss; she being accompanied by groups of genii, or children, in allusion to the rising generation, who offer consolation to her, by producing the trident and the rudder'.

On the front of the pedestal are inscribed the words: 'This statue in Honour of Admiral Lord Nelson Was Erected by the Inhabitants of Birmingham A.D. M.DCCCIX'. Around the whole, were placed iron palisadoes, 'in the form of bearing pikes connected by a twisted cable; and at each of the four corners is affixed a cannon erect, from which issues a lamp post, representing a cluster of pikes supporting a ship lantern'. Interestingly, Joseph Farror, an auctioneer who lived in the High Street, bequeathed sixpence a week 'to be paid for ever out of the rent of a house in Bradford Street', for the cleaning of the statue and its base.

Nelson's statue was sited in a conspicuous spot in that great triangle of space which had Saint Martin's Church as its base and which encompassed the outdoor markets of the Bull Ring. It was located opposite Bell Street, between the Market Hall and the Fish Market, and across the way from the appropriately named Nelson Passage in the lower end of the High Street.

After the 1960s redevelopment of the Bull Ring, Nelson's Statue was put in an obscure spot on the edge of the Inner Ring Road and above public lavatories. When it is put back to a fitting place of attention it should be done so with ceremony and honour, not only in respect for one of our greatest heroes but also for the Brummies who resolved to remember Lord Nelson so appropriately.

At the Heart of Things: Brum's Barrow Boys

Some days it was really hard dragging y'self out a bed so early in the morning. But it was no good moping about and moaning, you had to do it and that was that. You'd med y'r bed and y' had to lie on it and no-one but you had med the decision to pack up a good job in the factory and have a crack at a life in the open air in Brummagem's Bull Ring.

Mind you, often you thought to yourself that you was a cranky so and so for ever becoming a barrow boy – what, with having to get up and about when anyone in their right mind would still be a bed. And then, after a quick swill and a cup of char, having t' mek y'r way up to the wholesale markets and choose y'r produce for the day. Ah well said Nell, that's life and there was plenty that was worse off. Any road up, you always felt like this in the winter when y' had to trudge about in the dark mornings and it was s' parky that the frost bit into y'r hands and face and chapped them .

Darkie Morley is the chap standing on the right-hand side of this photograph which has been sent in by his son Mr F. Morley. Darkie was born in 1890 and was about 25 when this shot was taken. When he died aged 79 'he must have been one of the oldest hawkers at that time'. This is a cracking photograph showing Darkie and other traders standing by the old type of flat handcart from which the barrow boys used to sell.

Reg Huckfield now lives in Diss in Norfolk and only recently printed out a number of negatives which were taken about 1950 in the Bull Ring. This is one of them and it shows two of the lads who shifted the goods from the wholesale markets to the barrow boys in the Bull Ring.

Bill Searles is probably the oldest barrow boy left in the town. After his Mom's sad death, he left home aged fourteen and a half and six months later got his first hawker's badge and worked for a man called Smith who used to buy tomatoes and bananas. When Bill couldn't get a good pitch by Woolworth's, he would go round the streets 'shouting my eyeballs out. I used to earn enough money to pay for my rent and food'. Later, Bill borrowed money off Mr Smallwood, the owner of the coffee house in Dean Street where he lodged, to sell for himself. He recalls that 'I have bought 10 boxes of bananas for 10 shillings, one shilling a box. They were called eldoradoes. You bought for a shilling because they were a bit ripe but good enough to eat. There were 12 dozen bananas in a box and I sold them at 3d a dozen. That leaves me with £1 profit. I would pay my rent and food money and would finish with 7 shillings for myself and that was a lot of money in them days. I went about 3 days a week because you could not buy cheap fruit everyday.'

Tina Jones's great granddad was George 'Plimma' Harris. Where his nickname came from 'is anybody's guess, maybe it was something to do with his sparring as he used to be one of Bert Taylor's sparring partners'. Tina's dad remembers having to carry an enamel white billy can with the blue rim up to his Granddad in the Bull Ring: 'It was a full of tea with the odd tot of rum mixed in. He took it to his dad with a lunch parcel which was gratefully received on those cold market mornings'. Plimma was always dressed smart with a silk cravat, bowler hat and a flower in his crombie coat 'and shoes to see your face in'. He was real Brummie and true market trader.

Above all, it was the gloom which really med y' feel mardy, but a course, things really perked up in the summer and spring. Then y' couldn't wait to pull yerself out a bed and cop hold of a new day. The light seemed to bring you alive, as it did both the other traders and punters, and then y' set off gaily t' get y'r pitch sorted out.

Any road up, even in the winter, y' knew that y'r mood would change for the better s'never y' reached the Bull Ring and began to 'Alright' this chap and 'Ow do' that feller. That's when y' knew that you had med the right move to become a barrow boy. Because it was the people, your pals amongst the traders and the shoppers who kept drawing y' back to the hand carts and Spiceal Street.

As a barrow boy y' felt, and knew, that you was really at the heart of things. You were there right there in the middle of the city and y' could feel Brummagem, now and in the past and all its people, coursing through your body and soul. You'd challenge anybody not to perk up once their feet hit the cobblestones of the Bull Ring and you came close enough to Saint Martin's to draw in the smells and tastes of the fish, veges and fruit. You couldn't whack it and y'knew that there was no better spot on earth and no place where you'd rather be.

And for all the Bull Ring was s'busy and full of activity, there were some things that only the barrow boys and a few others knew about. Like the sight of all the hawkers gathering at the back of the markets at about half past six each morning. Whatever the weather, come wind, rain or shine, they'd be pulled tight in a bunch around two coppers – one of whom would dip the fingers of his right hand into a big old bag.

Each time he did so, his hand came back up with a brass badge. This was the hawker's licence, without which no barrow boy could trade. That draw was all important, because the first ones out of the bag had the best pitches up by the steps of Woolworth's, where the crowds of shoppers were at their greatest – attracted as they were by the nearby Market Hall and a variety of exciting shops.

Those barrow boys whose badges came out towards the end of the draw had to set up their hand carts further on down the hill, stretching into Jamaica Row. Here, away from the action, it was quieter and much harder to shift your goods. That's why y'didn't buy your stuff until the draw was med, because where y'r pitch was determined how much you'd lay out.

Some of the lads specialised in fruit, but him, his game was mixed salad, the likes of radishes, lettuces, celery, watercress and spring onions. After he'd got what he wanted, he'd head off to the sorting yard to swill the salad and then lay it out as good as he could on his cart. Now he was set for the day. All thoughts of his morning groans had flitted away as he got ready for the banter and the chatter, the larking about and the laughter. As soon as the first punter came to him, that's when he knew why he was a barrow boy in the Bull Ring.

Percy and Iris Moseley selling fruit from a barrow in the old Bull Ring in the 1950s. In 2000, Iris Moseley was drawn to one of my articles by the comments of a reader who remembered a glamorous market trader with 'lots of blonde hair and long red nails, selling vegetables'. That trader was Iris Moseley and she is running a stall to this day in the Bull Ring, having taken on the pitch from her father. In fact, 'the family name has been in the Bull Ring markets for over 200 years'.

Percy Moseley himself was a noted barrow boy of whom it was asserted that 'he could sell anything'. He had learned his trade from his father and uncle and from 1908 was selling fish, fruit, rabbits and poultry. Distinguished by his black trilby, once he sold more than 1,000 rabbits in a day at a price of 8d each. And it was Percy who sold the first Brazilian pineapples in Brum after the Second World War, at a time when such a fruit was rare and exotic. Huge crowds turned up to watch Percy flog the pineapples

Unable to find work after the First World War, Mr S. J. T. Grubb's father 'got a barrow and bought oranges for it which he took to the Bull Ring to sell. At that time we lived in a back-to-back house in Hurst Street so it was not far to walk. My father had to obtain a hawker's licence which was in the form of a brass badge. He did very well in this employment and as time went on he gradually had a lot of men working for him'. When Mr Grubb was about nine years of age, his mother also had a barrow from which she sold celery and lettuce. She had to wash the produce in cold water 'which was very hard work. By this time I too was involved in helping selling from the barrows. I never liked the work at all and to this day I cannot eat oranges as just the smell brings back memories from all those years ago!'

Laying the Wreath: The End of the Old Bull Ring

What more fitting place was there to lay a wreath in memory of the Old Bull Ring than old Nelson's Statue? He'd been there since 1809, having been unveiled just a couple of years after the Bull Ring of Memory had emerged from the clearance of decrepit houses in Spiceal Street, the Bull Ring and the bottom end of High Street. And now as that Bull Ring was to be thrown so swiftly into the past, his noble frame stood encased in rusty scaffolding and mucky planks of wood.

This is a cracking shot of the Bull Ring of Memory, the old Bull Ring as it was in the mid-1950s just before it was heaved out of history by the bulldozers of redevelopment. On the right, a bus is turning into Moor Street – on the corner of which is Oswald Bailey's store. Between here and the Times building, the clearance of other structures stresses that the radical transformation of the Bull Ring has begun.

It's obviously not a Tuesday, Thursday or Saturday because there are no stall holders selling poultry, rabbits, eggs, plants and shrubs – but even without these traders the vitality of the Bull Ring is clear. On the left-hand side, the barrow boys are lining Spiceal Street, down from Bell Street to Edgbaston Street and are pulling in a host punters. Between them and Woolworth's, the pavements are packed with shoppers – and across the way crowds have been drawn around what must be characters performing some act or other. You can pick out a circle of attentive folk directly beneath Nelson's Statue, whilst there is another big gathering of people keen to watch some more goings on closer to the telephone boxes.

The power of this photograph is similar to that of the superb painting by David Cox of the Bull Ring in the 1820s. With a heart-tugging insight, both capture not only the look of the Bull Ring but also its feel. Of course, the buildings of the Bull Ring were vital to its appeal but the most important aspect of the Bull Ring is that open space which came alive through its people – the traders, the street performers, the speakers, the shoppers. The people of Birmingham. They made the Bull Ring for the Bull Ring belonged to them.

A demonstration of strength by Tralavia the strongman in the Bull Ring, November 23, 1951. Tralavia is the man holding the rock whilst it is hit with a sledge hammer wielded with force by another man. The crowd watching the feat are gathered in front of the old Fish Market, next door to which is the premises of C. S. Hawkesford and Son, tobacconists. Three doors down in Spiceal Street was Woolworth's, whilst to the right of the crowd and not in shot was Nelson's Statue.

Keith Neale and his wife Maureen spotted this photo in one of my **Evening Mail** *articles and have dropped me a cracking letter telling me that there are two Irishmen watching the goings on. Second from the left in the front row and with a cigarette in his mouth is Chris Delaney. On his right and with a muffler wrapped round him is Christie Delaney. Chris Delaney was a relative of Maureen and she tells me that he was married to Nancy and they had five children: Christie, Jimmy, Desi, Vincent and Dolores. Unable to find work in Dublin, Chris came to Brum in the early 1950s as he knew that Maureen's father, William Morgan, was already working here. Another Dub, Bill helped Chris to get work at Wright's Ropes in Garrison Street and digs in nearby Victoria Street.*

Later on, Chris moved on to a steel cutting yard in Bordesley Green where unfortunately he lost four fingers in a machinery accident. Chris then returned to Ireland. All his sons followed him to Birmingham in search of work, although some of them did go back home. Chris often visited the Bull Ring for as Maureen states, it had 'entertainment and cheap shopping, as it was a very lonely existence living in digs with his family across the Irish Sea. On Sundays they would attend Mass at Saint Anne's in Deritend before taking Sunday lunch at Bill's home. Chris regularly sent money home to Nancy until he returned after the accident.'

Tralavia was just one a of a number of well-known entertainers who sought to make a living from doing this and that in the Bull Ring. There was the escapologist, who tied himself in chains, and the fire eater. And in the inter-war years people such as this were joined by the sad figures of ex-servicemen maimed in the First World War who sat on the edge of the pavements in Spiceal Street playing dulcimers and other instruments so as to gain a few coppers from sympathetic passers-by.

That day, September 11, 1959, a number of stall holders decided that they wanted to show their regret at the passing of their world. So they clambered between the poles and held up to the cameras their tribute to their pal, the old Bull Ring. Not surprisingly there were no officials there. What need of them was there? For the Bull Ring had never been owned by the officials, it had belonged to the people of Brum and that day the stallholders were representing the people.

It was one of those warm days you often get in late September and some of the stallholders were in their shirt sleeves. And as the sun shone down on them they must have thought why? Why was it all changing? Why were they going to be moved away from their pitches? Why had the council given up on the old Bull Ring? No-one had asked the stallholders, the barrow boys or the flower sellers for their opinions about the changes which were rushing through Brum. No-one had consulted them about their wishes. Most of all, no-one had asked them if they minded if their way of life would be chucked away.

Alan Sollinger came up to the West Midlands from London in the mid-1960s. He worked the markets in the Black Country and then took a pitch in the new Bull Ring outdoor market. He stood close to the pedestrian way which went under the Inner Ring Road and quickly gained a fine reputation as a pitcher, someone who is able to draw in the crowds through swift speech, banter with the crowds and showmanship. Selling quality products such as towels at keen prices, Alan became a major trader in the new Bull Ring. Here he has pulled an edge, a crowd, and is now tempting the punters to buy his goods. Although he is no longer trading in the Bull Ring, Alan recalls those days with great fondness and in his present business he continues to adhere to the principles he upheld then. Now he runs Snax Café in New Canal Street, where good food is served at the most reasonable of prices.

This shot from the later 1960s shows Nelson's Statue on the right, overlooking the Inner Ring Road as it sped down from Moor Street Station. Close to the statue was a carousel, followed by the line of shops at the back of the shot. Like the stalls below them, these premises have been demolished as part of another redevelopment of the Bull Ring.

The decision to do away with the Old Bull Ring had been taken by planners, councillors and developers who were certain that they knew best. And what they were sure of was that Brum needed high-rise buildings, indoor shopping centres with escalators and fancy mod cons, and wide roads under which pedestrians would be forced to walk.

What they never even thought about was that Brum could have become a go-ahead city imitating the American model and still kept the old Bull Ring. That triangular space of land between Saint Martin's and the bottom end of New Street could have been a major feature of a new Brum which yet grasped proudly its roots. But that idea never had a chance and the Bull Ring was changed irrevocably.

In 1962 the outdoor market was re-opened in the new Bull Ring. No longer did the barrow boys line Spiceal Street and no longer did the stall holders put up their trestles about Nelson's Statue. Instead, everyone traded from permanent stalls. Those folk who worked those stalls fought hard to make the new market a place open to the folk of Brum. They fought and they won. People continued to flock to the outdoor markets, for good quality products at keen prices and sold often by bantering, bubbling characters. Even though many aspects of the old Bull Ring were missed, the new outdoor market grabbed the affections of Brummies.

The market traders did a wonderful job. Now as that new Bull Ring itself has been reinvigorated in an exciting way it is essential that those traders should be given a key role in the forging of a new Bull Ring. For no-one should forget that Brummagem began as a market town and throughout our history the market traders have been at the core of our being.

A Vision of America: The 1960s Bull Ring

On the May 29, 1964 Prince Philip, the Duke of Edinburgh, opened the new £8 million multi-level complex of the Bull Ring Centre. To his right is the Lord Mayor of Birmingham, Alderman Frank Price, and Sir Herbert Manzoni, the City Engineer and Surveyor. This event must have been one of the most satisfying moments in the life of Sir Herbert Manzoni. He was a man who was used to highpoints in his career, but on

This wonderful photograph was sent in to me several years ago by Gerald Scane. It shows the construction of the Inner Ring Road and emphasises how that project bulldozed across the old street pattern of Birmingham and so placed the Bull Ring outside the official city centre. Nelson's Statue can be seen still standing opposite what had been Bell Street. To its left, the Fish Market has been cleared already, and within a short time the same fate will overwhelm the block of shops which includes Woolworth's; to the right of Nelson, the Market Hall is about to be demolished; whilst the lorries are shifting the earth from what had been the lower part of High Street.

The Inner Ring Road was a vital part of the vision which was to force from history the old Bull Ring of Brum. It was a vision which had no place for short streets, old buildings and traditional ways but which fastened on wide freeways, high-rise structures and new ideas. Old Brummagem would be chucked into the miskin of history and in its place would emerge a city in the sky – just like those in America, the land of the future.

As early as the last years of the war, detailed plans had been drawn up for the construction of an Inner Ring Road and in 1946 they were approved by Parliament. Granted wide powers, Birmingham Council began work on its flagship project in 1957 and within two years the new road system had felled its way from the Horse Fair to Queen's Drive and had begun to swoop down on the stretch of land up to Carrs Lane. In its wake, the Inner Ring Road brought other major changes – not least the obliteration of the old Bull Ring.

Looking up from Park Street to the Bull Ring Centre, in front of which are the outdoor traders. Taken probably in the late 1960s or early 1970s, this photographs highlights the triumph of the new over the old. There is nothing here which could connect the modern Bull Ring with its forerunner. In the centre, the bus is about to turn left on to the Inner Ring Road, roughly at the spot where Nelson's Statue had been placed, and along what had been Bell Street. The Market Hall once stood along the line of the Mann's advert, whilst Phillips Street would have run on the other side of the beerglass. The Rotunda rises up over what had been the bottom part of New Street and the upper part of Worcester Street. Built in 1964, the Rotunda cost £1,000,000 and gained the affection of Brummies like myself who grew up from the 1960s onwards.

this day it must have seemed that everything he had striven for was about to be achieved. For here he was, he was proud to accompany Prince Philip who was entrusted with the official opening of the new Bull Ring Centre – a place which epitomised Birmingham's thirst to become the most modern of modern cities.

Manzoni had come to Birmingham in 1935 when he had been appointed City Engineer and Surveyor. Swiftly, he came to exert a tremendous influence over leading councillors through the clarity of his ideas and the strength of his character. It was his vision to clear Birmingham of its back-to-back houses and develop new towns in which there would be clear zones for work, living, leisure and transport. And it was his

A panoramic shot of the new Bull Ring in the 1970s. This picture emphasises how the Inner Ring Road cut off many of the outdoor traders and Saint Martin's from the official city centre. Behind the church is the Row and the squat structure of the Wholesale Market. As can be seen, the redevelopment of the Bull Ring area was comprehensive. It led not only to the opening of the Bull Ring Centre but also to a new open air market. Located in permanent stalls which began in front of Saint Martin's and spread under the Inner Ring Road towards New Street and High Street, this market was ready for business from June 1962. With 150 covered stalls and pitches, it was open for six days a week for the sale of fruit, vegetables and miscellaneous goods – whilst flower sellers lined the route of the old Spiceal Street up from the entrance of the new Market Hall.

Across Edgbaston Street, more traders could be found outside the Rag Market – although from 1977 this area was designated as the Row Market where traders specialised in selling clothes to teenagers. The Rag Market itself was based in the Saint Martin's Retail Market. Begun in 1938, the war stopped the completion of the project and it was not finally finished until 1957.

Open three days a week, at first the Rag Market shared the building with farmers, growers and wholesale horticultural traders. However, from 1976 these people were accommodated in a modern Wholesale Markets Precinct which was opened on October 13 by Her Royal Highness, Princess Anne. Covering 21 acres, the development was dominated by a large Horticultural Market but also it included a Meat Market, Fish Market, Poultry Market and Growers' Market – at which produce was sold directly from lorries.

Birmingham's wholesale markets remain crucial to the well being of the city and future plans for the Bull Ring and the markets must ensure that the city continues to be a major national centre for wholesale trading in fruit, vegetables, meat, fish and poultry.

vision to gird Birmingham City Centre with a road around which traffic would flow freely and which would signify Birmingham's determination to slough off its nineteenth-century heritage and to welcome not only the twentieth-century but also the twenty-first century.

Manzoni found a powerful ally in Alderman Frank Price. One of the leading figures in the post-war Labour group, he was chairman of the important Public Works Committee – under the auspices of which much of the redevelopment of Birmingham was carried on. Later knighted for his services to Birmingham, Sir Frank Price himself had lived in bad housing and was committed passionately to making life better for the working class of the city. Today it is easy for a historian such as myself to dismiss the post-Second World War redevelopment of Birmingham as a mistake, but at the time Sir Frank Price and his colleagues were driven forward by a desire to build a better world and to do so quickly.

There can be little doubt that they had to act fast. By the early 1950s, the traffic problems in the city were so bad that Birmingham was grinding to a halt and there was a desperate need for up-to-date shopping facilities. The Inner Ring Road and a new Bull Ring seemed to be part of the answer to these needs – and only with hindsight did it become obvious that Brum lost something special when the old Bull Ring was cleared.

The Bull Ring Centre scheme itself was seen by many people as brilliant in its conception. It covered much of the four acres leased from the City by the Laing Development Corporation Ltd at a ground rent of about £110,000 a year for 99 years. In total, the developed area of the Centre was 1,000,000 square feet, of which 350,000 square feet was retail trading space, and it drew to itself the superlatives of its supporters. Declared to be the 'world's most advanced shopping centre', it incorporated a new market hall which was claimed to be the finest retail market area in Europe and perhaps the world.

What, then, did the new Bull Ring Centre include? In its 'air-conditioned comfort', shoppers could choose 'between the relative merits of the department store, the supermarket, the traditional market stall and any one of its 140 individual shops'. In addition to these facilities, there were restaurants, cafes, coffee bars, pubs, gardens, fashion parades, exhibitions, special facilities for children, a rest room and first-aid post, a central parcels depot where shoppers could leave their purchases until they were ready to leave, garages, offices and a large bus station – now the temporary home of the Rag Market.

The focal point of the Bull Ring Centre was the Centre Court, a space of 1,280 square feet which boasted two escalators and a specially-designed ceiling. Here it was intended to create all 'the interest and gaiety of a French boulevard' through the serving of light refreshments under bright sunshades and alongside sparkling fountains, blossoming trees and shining marble walls. It is hard now to grasp the optimism which led journalists and commentators to wax lyrical about its size, its look, and its features. Sadly, that optimism soon drained away as the Bull Ring Centre with its glass tiles, exposed aggregate concrete, synthetic laminates and plastic rock walls came to symbolise what many people regarded as the failings of the architecture of the 1960s. For those of us in the late 1970s and onwards who saw the Bull Ring Centre as a tired building, it is hard to grasp the optimism which led journalists and commentators to wax lyrical about its size, its look, and its features. In the year 2000, that building was cleared and the traders were moved into a new Market Hall at the bottom end of Edgbaston Street. Here they continue to do what they have done so well for 165 years – humorously and happily serve the people of Birmingham. Still, for the success of Birmingham, the present redevelopment of the Bull Ring has to be longer-lasting and to do so it must incorporate the memory of the past as much as the thinking of the present and the vision of the future.

Chapter 2:

Brummies

Brummies Helping Themselves: The Birmingham Hospital Saturday Fund

For those millions of people across the world who have been drawn in by the enchanted world of Middle Earth in Tolkien's *The Lord of the Rings*, Sam Gamgee, is the brave, loyal and dogged man-servant of Frodo Baggins – the 'hero' of this fantasy which features hobbits, dwarves, elves, orcs and other mythological creatures.

But for Brummies of the mid-1800s, Sam Gamgee was a real person, a dedicated surgeon who laboured determinedly to improve the health of the working class. It was he who invented what was known locally as Gamgee tissue – cotton wool – and it was he who founded the Birmingham Hospital Saturday Fund, one of the most important institutions in the history of our city.

Born Joseph Sampson Gamgee in 1828 in Italy, he was already a distinguished surgeon when he came to Birmingham in 1857 to work at the Queen's Hospital – later the well-loved 'Acci', the Accident Hospital. In 1868, Sampson Gamgee investigated the problems of the outpatient department and found that it needed urgent improvement. There was too little space, a lack of toilets and no opportunity for isolating contagious diseases. These difficulties were made worse by tiny, gloomy and poorly ventilated dressing rooms.

Money was needed desperately to improve these inadequate and potentially unhealthy conditions, but there were no funds to spare. The state took no interest in supporting hospitals and consequently their income came only from the donations of the wealthy and the fees charged to outpatients.

But fees caused severe problems. It was hard for the poor to come up with the tanner or shilling needed for medical attention – and if they did so, something else had to be cut back on, such as food. And if they couldn't get hold of silver, then illnesses were neglected and became worse.

Alert to these harsh realties, Gamgee came up with the idea of Hospital Saturday. He noticed that the local churches has an annual Hospital Sunday, the collections from which went to local hospitals, and so the collection he inspired would be specifically for the extension of the Queen's Hospital. So soon as ever the idea was made public 'a number of foremen and artisans tendered an offer of assistance to raise the necessary funds'. A working men's' fund was set up quickly and 800 representatives collared strenuously to raise money. The working people of Brum responded enthusiastically and generously to the appeal and in 1871 the extension to the Queen's was opened.

This is a smashing shot of collectors for the Hospital Saturday fund setting themselves up at a stall in the middle of the horse road and behind the two coppers. Taken in 1893 it shows the bottom end of Corporation Street, just by the junction with New Street. On the right are the premises of Geo. Dean, tailors, above which are Prince's Chambers – which were filled with a variety of shipping agents, stock brokers, consulting engineers and other professionals. Further up, the canopies indicate a number of shops below Warwick Chambers .

Mr H. Woodcock tells me that his wife's grandfather was one of the original members who set up the Birmingham Hospital Saturday Fund 'and would be seen on Nechells Green to collect the money due'. His name was John Muirhead and with his pals H. Priddy and Thomas Winship, he attended the first meeting of the Fund representing the workpeople of the Metropolitan Railway Carriage and Wagon Company in Saltley. Subsequently, John Muirhead was appointed to the executive committee of the Hospital Saturday Collection Fund, was president of the Nechells collecting area for thirteen years and was works secretary to the fund for 22 years. A staunch working-class Liberal, John was a man who strove might and main on behalf of his fellows and was prominent in the agitation to get a nine-hour working day.

Louis Power's father, William Charles Power, was another stalwart of the BHSF. He was honorary secretary of the Fund for many years until his death in 1947 'and I understand he may have been a founder member of the Fund. I well remember, as a child, that the family were always told to be very quiet on Sunday afternoons because father was "doing his writing", that is, he was writing up his reports and minutes in his beautiful "copper plate" writing. He also spent hours walking around the locality (Ward End) mostly in the evenings visiting those persons who had applied to go to one of the convalescent homes. I often accompanied him on these walks.' When William Charles Power died 'The Fund had many oak seats made and each had a plate fixed to them with his name inscribed. These were then presented to the convalescent homes. I wonder if any still survive?'

But Sampson Gamgee did not stop there. He appreciated the desire amongst working-class folk for good medical facilities and he also knew that they wanted to help themselves. Thus in 1873 and through his drive, the Hospital Saturday Fund was set up. Its first collection was on March 15 and the proceeds were shared amongst the local hospitals.

A year later, the collections were supplemented with penny a week subscriptions. Then in 1891, the secretary of the Fund, William T. Smedley, proposed that the organisation should set up its own convalescent homes, nursing service and surgical aid department. As a result, the Fund became the Birmingham Hospital Saturday Fund and within a year it had opened Ty-Y-Coed, the Alfred Stokes Memorial Home, close to Llandudno.

From its beginnings, the BHSF has been a dynamic and progressive organisation which has adapted successfully to changing circumstances and the needs of its members. In a society where the National Health Service now provides health care, the BHSF no longer makes donations to local hospitals, and although it maintains one convalescent home its main purpose now is as a provider of health insurance for more than 300,00 people. Proud of its history, the BHSF will continue to be an innovative and forward-looking body which seeks to do the best for its members.

Mabel Ford went to the BHSF convalescent home at Marle Hall in Llandudno in June 1941 and is the youngster sitting on the arm of the bench, fourth from the right on the back row. She was fifteen years old and had been sent for recuperation after having appendicitis. Mabel recollects that 'we all had a grand time for the 2 weeks we were there and all felt much better in health on returning home. Up the road from Marle Hall was the men's convalescent home, it was called Tyn-y-Coed ... There was a house up the road, just an ordinary private house where you could go for a cup of tea and the lady told you your fortune from the tea leaves. Everybody called the house "the widow's" and all the men and women from the homes went to "the widow's" for a cuppa.' Mabel joined the BHSF when she started work at fourteen and paid a 1d a week and she remains a member.

*A lovely photo of Brummie women at Kewstoke Convalescent Home for Women in May 1962. Thanks to June Depper, whose mom, Jessie Depper nee Green, is on the photo. Sheila Harries was 'emotionally happy' when she saw this shot in the **Evening Mail** as it includes her mother, Mrs L. M. Codling of Ladywood. Born in 1907, Mrs Codling was at Kewstoke following the sad death of her husband. Unfortunately, Mrs Codling herself died five years ago but Sheila is 'sure she would have been delighted that the photo was shown. Indeed it was a wonderful surprise for myself and her grandchildren. Many, many thanks June Depper.'*

Opened in 1932, Kewstoke is at Weston super Mare which was believed to be 'unrivalled for its fine recuperative air'. Set in wide grounds it is two miles from Sand Bay and is approached through woods. Mrs J. Capewell recalls Kewstoke well. In 1937 when she was fourteen she was very ill with double pneumonia and 'the doctor said I must go to convalescent. So thanks to my father being in the Birmingham Saturday Hospital Fund I was able to go to Kewstoke.'

Betty Grattage nee White is another person who believes firmly that the BHSF is 'a fantastic organisation'. When she first started work contributions were deducted from wages at source and when she got sick in the summer of 1953 the doctor asked her if she was a member of the BHSF. When she told him she was he recommended two weeks convalescence at Kewstoke. Betty and a girl called Christine from Kings Heath were the two youngest at the home and they were put in twin room on the top floor. They were nicknamed the terrible twins but 'what a happy two weeks we all had. Oh, of course there were Rules and Regulations which had to be obeyed otherwise Matron would deal with you. There was "Charlie's Cafe" at the bottom of the drive where we all used to meet up for refreshments etc. He had lovely gardens with a swing seat and deck chairs. The sea being just minutes. The airs was so fresh and clean. I should think we all benefited from being there.' Thankfully, Kewstoke continues its important role for the modern BHSF.

A Woman Who Gave: Elizabeth Green and Her Mission

Everyone who met her declared that she was both a lady and a Christian woman. And so she was. Elizabeth Green was imbued with a deep sense of the necessity of giving to others. Throughout her life she reached out to the poor and the needy not – because she wanted to be seen as a lady bountiful but because it was her duty to do so as a follower of Jesus. And through her holding out her hands and her heart, she touched the lives of hundreds of people and did good.

Elizabeth Green, the founder of the Elizabeth Green Mission in Alcester Street, Deritend. Charles Evans stresses that this lady was a dedicated Christian and had hoped to become a missionary abroad 'but when this became impossible she turned to the task of helping the poor and illiterate and she used the Bible and Hymn books to this end. She had a friend, Miss James, who helped with great dedication and who later became Mrs Edmonds. She had a son James and he carried on the work after his mother died. In the early days there was a caretaker, but as the local population was rehoused, attendance dropped and vandalism added to the troubles of the mission. For a long time Jim Edmonds ran the mission single handed and often had to go early on Sunday mornings to light an antiquated stove before a few people turned up. Ultimately it had to close and thus came to an end.' These notes were passed to Charles by Jim, 'to whom I am slightly related by marriage'.

Elizabeth Green grew up in her aunt's house on the Pershore Road and as a girl she was an active member of St Luke's Church on Bristol Street. As she grew older, she felt compelled to do more for those who were less fortunate than herself and so she brought together a few lads in the Boys' Night Shelter in Bradford Street. Soon after, she and some friends began a Mission for Poor Children at Chapel House in Deritend and as the project grew it was moved to Warwick Street.

This work with poorer youngsters led to the founding of the Children's Scripture Union Mission in Alcester Street, Deritend – the place which would become known as the Elizabeth Green Mission. The woman who inspired it ensured that its work would not be connected with any particular sect. And as well as drawing people in to the buildings of the Mission she went out and about to conduct dinner hour services amongst young women who worked in local factories and was also a keen member of the Birmingham Young Women's Christian Association and of the Children's Service Union.

Elizabeth Green died on September 1, 1917 at her house at 118, Moseley Road, Highgate. She was 56, and as reported in the *Mail*, it was believed that her fatal illness had been brought on 'by her self-sacrifice, for she gave untiringly of her time to any and all who were in need. She was always ready to answer the call of sickness, and on many occasions tended a bedside for many nights in succession. A call for help at any hour of day or night brought immediate response.'

Without its founder, the Elizabeth Green Mission may have floundered. That it did not is a testament to how well she had built the fellowship amongst those with whom she worked and worshipped. Four years after her death, the members of the Mission raised £1,200 to rebuild and renovate part of the Mission Rooms. Everyone got involved, from four year olds upwards, in repairing floors, match-boarding the walls, mending benches, doing the gas fittings, scrubbing, cleaning and varnishing.

Younger members of the Elizabeth Green Mission posing for a photo in the early 1900s. The first man on the left is L. W.. Silverthorn; next to him is George Billington senior; the man fourth from the left is Harry Gibson; and fifth and sixth from the left are Tom Tonks and Ted McDonald. The third lady on the left (standing) is Rose Bartlett, who married George Billington, and on her right is her sister Ada, who married Harry Gibson. The couple seated on the left are Mr and Mrs Orme.

This photo has been sent in by George and John Billington, whose father, George, is featured. With Harry Gibson, they 'were two of the boys that Elizabeth Green got together and from childhood and youth were members of the Mission'. George the younger was born in 1915 'and was taken to the Mission as a very young baby then four years later my brother was born and he went to the Mission – like me he was carried in my mother's arms. My father and his boyhood friend met two sisters – the one became my mother, the other my aunt and they also went to the Mission with my Dad and my Uncle Harry.'

The Mission was like a second home to the Billingtons and other families and they lived by its teaching. Indeed, George himself also met his wife at the Mission. Even though, it has been closed since 1966, George, John and a few others 'meet occasionally and talk of our Mission and what great times we had and our new friends look in wonderment at our stories and say what a marvellous place it was and right they are. We do miss our Mission.'

The same commitment characterised the members of the Mission in the succeeding years. They were determined to do whatever they could to make life better not only for themselves but also for the youngsters who attended children's services. To this end they organised an adult school, women's fellowship, a benevolent section, a Sickness and Dividend Fund, a Band of Hope, a Youth Club, a men's Club, Girl Guides, a children's mid-week club and an annual outing to the Lickeys as well as a Christmas Party for the youngsters.

Sadly in 1966, the work of the Mission ended. The clearance of the back-to-backs in Highgate and the movement of so many of its people to outer city area meant that numbers attending the Mission had dwindled to a number too low for it to continue. Yet if the Mission is no more then the work of Elizabeth Green and the communion of its people remain in the souls of many.

This photo of Brenda M. Hawkings shows members of the Women's Fellowship of the Mission on holiday at Penmaenmawr in Wales about 1958. Brenda was a member of the Elizabeth Green Mission from the 1940s until it closed, at which time the proceeds from the sale of the property were divided between two charities – one of which was the Children's Hospital. At that time Dorothy Allely was the president and Jim Edmonds was the treasurer. Amongst past presidents brought to mind by Brenda are Frances Allesley, the mother of the last president; Arthur Churchill, who had a chemist shop in Cotteridge and who always used to give a half-a-crown to the men lodging in Rowton House who used to wait for him every Sunday; and Mrs Edmonds, the mother of the treasurer, who led the Women's Fellowship and who organised the annual holidays to Wales.

Mrs Edmonds is sitting second from the left in the front row. Next to her is Mrs Frances Alleley and at the end of the row is Miss Daisy Richards, a school teacher who had 'well over 50 children in her class and who saved a few pence throughout the year to give the children a Christmas party'. Other stalwarts of the mission were Miss Edna Hughes the organist, Ted Langford, superintendent of the Sunday evening service, Tom Hughes, Fred Orme, Harry Bagley, Frank Fitzpatrick and the Fox family.

The Gentleman Champion from Ashted: Jack Hood

That punch changed the course of his life – and it all came about because he'd overslept. Just fourteen years old in 1916, Jack Hood was grafting in a weighbridge office and like other working chaps in Ashted, a knocker-up woke him for work. That morning, the gentle taps on his window roused him at half-past five, but after calling out that he'd heard the knocks, Jack closed his eyes.

When he awoke, he met some chaps in their late teens and early twenties. Despite his youth, Jack knocked about with them and they headed for Silk's coffee house for tea in a glass mug and a chat about pigeon racing. Then someone suggested a game of cards. Playing for money was illegal and so Jack and his mates headed for an old brewhouse nearby, where, hidden from the local coppers, they got stuck into a game of pontoon.

After losing a few hands, Jack tumbled that the cards were marked and when he dealt he thought he'd give the others their comeuppence. One of the fellers had a five-card trick, totalling 21, the most you could get. Jack turned over his first two cards. They were a nine and a deuce – making eleven. He twisted two more cards – a four and five – which took him to twenty. On that, Jack should have paid twenty-ones but he got cute and spotted that the next card on the deck was marked an ace. With a score of one that would take him to 21 and allow him, as the bank, to win. Acting surprised, Jack twisted the ace and the next minute he was on the floor, felled by a punch from the bloke with the five-card trick.

Hoping for sympathy when he got home, Jack showed his dad the cut he'd got on his chin. His father wasn't impressed that Jack hadn't fought back – but the following Saturday he bought his son a pair of boxing gloves and began to teach him to box. Jack then joined the Gasworks Recreation Club at Saltley in 1919 and after that trained at 'The Met', but his first proper fight was at the Midland Carriage Works in Washwood Heath. He won on points and received a small silver medal with a gold centrepiece. But because he'd taken part in a professional show, he was temporarily suspended by the Amateur Boxing Association.

The day before the suspension ended, Jack went to the boxing gaff of Tom Thomas on the Ladypool Road, Sparkbrook, where he stood in for another fighter. It was another professional bout and Jack was spotted by an amateur referee who warned him he'd be in trouble. There and then Jack resolved to become a professional and picked up the twenty-five bob he was owed for the fight.

Once again, Jack harked to the words of his dad who told him 'I shall never interfere with you, but I want you to remember this, don't get hit if you can help it, and if you do get hit don't squeal'. They were words which were imprinted indelibly upon Jack's mind and he held to them true and fast.

Jack's career really began in 1923 when he beat Kid Swaffer on points. He won five more fights that year, and another ten in 1924 – amongst them that against Tom Whitehouse which gave Jack the Midlands Welterweight Championship. By 1925, Jack was featuring on bills throughout England and out of nineteen fights he lost only one and drew two. Poised for boxing greatness, Jack Hood won the British Welterweight Championship on May 31, 1926 when he outpointed Harry Mason in a twenty-round contest at Holland Park.

Two months later, the Ashted lad successfully defended the title against the former champion and then headed for the States. In those days, it was felt that if he were to win, then a foreigner had to knock out an American boxer. So it proved for Jack, who showed his class when he drew one fight, with another getting a 'no decision'. Returning home, Jack continued to dominate the British welter-weight scene and after defeating Alf Mancini in June 1928 he won the Londsale Belt outright. Seeking other challenges, Jack moved up and took on Len Harvey for the British middle-weight title. In three hard-fought bouts, Jack lost two on points and drew the other. Refocusing on his own division, in May 1933, Jack Hood took the European Welterweight title.

What a cracking shot of Jack Hood taken at Walford Road in 1933. Thanks to Bill Shreeves and June Eastlake. Jack is standing third from the right and to his right are Billy Welsh and the boxing promoter, Ted Salmon. To his left are Arthur Stratton, match maker, and Stoker Reynolds, his opponent from Portsmouth. The fight took place on March 13 and was for the British welterweight title. Jack won the contest and was to be undefeated champion at that weight.

Interestingly, back on Monday June 25, 1928, Jack had defended his title successfully against Alf Mancini at Perry Barr Greyhound Racing Track. He won on points in a fifteen-round contest. The boxing manager of the bout was the well known racecourse bookie and boxing man, Ted Salmon; whilst one of the supporting fights was refereed by Owen Moran. Originally from Summer Lane, in his heyday, Owen had been a great boxer and many people declare that pound for pound he was the toughest boxer in the world. Also on the bill were Bert and Jack Kirby, Charlie Baxter, Archie Woodbine, Sam Shaw and P. O. Firth.

A customer admires Jack Hood's Lonsdale Belt in the 'Bell Inn' at Tanworth -in-Arden, 1968.

One Sunday, Mrs P. Davies was in the front room of her gran's house·in Denbigh Street, Bordesley Green when 'Jack Hood walked in, straight past me into the back room where my gran was peeling potatoes. He was wearing a black trilby and a long black overcoat. I didn't know who he was at the time as I must have been eight or nine years old. I remember when Jack Hood was leaving the house I went to the door and saw him getting into a big black car which was parked about two doors away from my gran's house. The car had a big, wide step. My mother told me that she believed that Jack Hood was my dad's cousin.'

William Hall was very pleased to hear that I would be writing about 'Gentleman Jack' – 'a lovely man and so respected. There will never be his like again.' William's dad had worked with Jack Hood at Samuel Heath's in Leopold Street and Jack himself became very friendly with Dennis Heath. In later years, William 'used to love visiting Jack's pub and being allowed to go into the house to see the Lonsdale Belt on display there'. Jack Hood's gentlemanliness is emphasised by Mr V. Smith. On one occasion he was sent to take milk to a newly-built house in Sarehole Road, Hall Green, but his vehicle ran out of fuel and he had come out with no money. Seeing a car outside a house 'I knocked to ask for help. The owner came to the door in singlet and shorts. He loaned me money and told me a can was in the dicky seat of his car and to put the money under the mat when I returned it. Some days later, informing a customer, I saw the man passing with his Airedale dog and I was informed that he was Jack Hood.'

Mr J. H. Beckstein was in the Air Training Corps in 1941-2 and was stationed in the 'Sun Insurance Offices' in Hall Green, where Jack Hood used to come to train the lads in boxing on the roof of the building. He was a marvellous person who was extremely fit. When Jack Suckling and his mates were lads and keen followers of boxing, they had a phrase, 'cut me 'air like Jack Hood's'; and Hilda Burnett recalls that when Jack Hood was boxing at the 'Embassy' in Walford Road, Sparkbrook, her mother would 'load up her barrow with extra oranges knowing there would be a full house. Off she would trundle, all the way up to the Stratford Road to the said place and stand outside selling the fruit.' Hilda also mentions that her mom knew Jack's brother, Tom, who worked at the Hippodrome.

Robert W. Barnes was introduced to Jack shortly before the boxer's death in 1992 and spent what must have been the best part of an hour chatting over the time he had spent in the ring and at the 'Bell': 'I remember Jack was propped up against the kitchen sink, with me up at the gas cooker! Well, it was where the beer was! Jack was a wonderful man, with all the time in the world for you. A true gentleman.'

Jack Hood retired from boxing in 1935. He never boxed as an amateur and he was never knocked out. He stood upright and boxed in the classic English way. So great was his fame that the Prince of Wales (later the Duke of Windsor) asked especially to see him box. Skilled, astute and clever, Jack Hood was most of all a gentleman who gained the respect of all who watched him and met him.

A smashing shot of Jack Hood (right) in his later life. On the left is George Morgan, a well-known bookie from Highgate and an amateur boxer of distinction. When I was a youngster, George used to help out Our Dad settling bets in our betting shop on the Stoney Lane and he used to entrance me with the stories of his numerous fights and the boxers he'd fought against. Next to George is Norman Hall and alongside him is Norman Gibbons, a man noted for his writings on old-time boxers and for his support of the Birmingham Old Boxers Association. Third from the right stands Ted Biddles, who managed Hogon Kid Bassey when he became world champion as Nigeria gained independence and who also managed Johnny Prescott, Jack Bodell, Richard Dunne and Brian Cartwright. And standing to the left of Jack Hood is Arnie Hall, who sent me this photo and who himself did stirling work for the old boxers of Brum.

Labouring for the Rights of Workers: Brummie Trade Unionists

As a kid he'd always been clammed. Often the only thing he had to eat all day was a piece of lard or a mess of sop – stale bread mashed up with the drippings from the tea pot. Many times there wornt even that in the house and so with other ragged kids he traipsed to the factory gates, to catch the blokes and wenches who were knocking off. It was a heart-wrenching sight, them youngsters calling out 'Ave yer any bread, mister? Ave yer any bread, miss?' What little was left from their dinners the workers doled out, remembering that 'there but for the Grace of God go I'.

Mind you, by the time he was six he was hard at collar himself, turning a wheel at a rope spinner's in Vauxhall. It was mighty work, twelve hours a day Monday to Friday. Even on Saturday, when he finished early he had no chance of dashing about outside his house in Farm Street, Hockley. No, he couldn't play tipcat, glarneys or acky-one-two-three. He had to go to a barber's and lather the faces of the chaps who wanted a shave – as he did again Sunday morning.

Childhood was something for the kids of the rich. Will Thorne and his mates had neither childish things nor childish thoughts. Little grown-ups they were with responsibilities way beyond their years. No wonder that as he toiled, Will railed against the hardships of his people. As he grew older, he went from job to job, always seeking to improve not only his pay but also his position. From the rope mill, he moved on to the Small Heath brick works, and after that he had spells as a plumber's mate, a lath splitter, a cow and pig-hair dresser, a brass roller, a nut and bolt tapper, a builder's labourer and a navvy.

But it was when he was employed at the Saltley Gas Works that Will Thorne started to think about what he could do to change things for himself and his fellow workers. The thing which pushed him into action was the back-breaking shift system. A fortnight of day work ended at 6 o'clock on a Sunday evening and straightaway the same set of lads began two weeks of nights. That change-over meant they grafted for a full 24 hours. Thorne called a meeting of the stokers to press for the abolition of Sunday work. He strove to get them to back him and when they did, he went off to see the chief engineer. The gaffer raved up and down the room, telling them to sling their hook if they didn't like things. Will didn't back down and a couple of weeks later, his tummy doing gambols, he heard that the men had won their battle.

Later Will Thorne moved to London where in 1889 he was one of the leading figures in the formation of the Gas Workers and General Labourers Union of Great Britain and Ireland. But he wasn't the only major trade unionist to come from Brum. One of his contemporaries was William John Davis. He, too, had begun to labour while still a child and he, too, had sworn that he would fight to stop other children having to experience the same ordeals as those he had gone through.

Starting out in the printing game, Davis shifted into the brass trade as a teenager during the 1860s. It was an exciting time for trade unionists. The Trades Union Congress was set up and new unions were springing up everywhere. Davis was swept

Grading Stamps of the National Society of Brassworkers and Metal Mechanics, 1914.

Striking workers, probably from the Metropolitan Railway and Carriage Works in Saltley, holding their strike boxes in High Street, Saltley in 1908.

Charles W. Bateman's great uncle, Henry Simpson, 'progressed from being a child nailmaker to becoming a prominent trade union official and Alderman of the City of Birmingham'. Born in 1866 in Bromsgrove, he was the first son of William and Sarah (nee Crump) and as a child made nails with his parents. When he was fourteen, he went to live with an uncle, Henry Crump, 'who was keeping a coffee shop in Saltley. Henry Crump was a well known Liberal worker who served on the Aston Board of Guardians until his death in 1897.'

After three years, Henry Simpson returned to Bromsgrove to make nails but 'owing to the poor state of the nailmaking industry at that time, he decided to return to Birmingham where he spent the rest of his life'. For nineteen years, he worked at the Saltley Gas Works 'where he joined the Amalgamated Society of Gas, Municipal and General Workers on the day it was formed in 1889. He took an active part in its work, being President of the Saltley Branch. In 1894 he became President of the Society, and the following year he was elected its first paid organiser. In 1907, he became General Secretary, and when it was amalgamated with the National Union of General and Municipal Workers in 1921, he was appointed Financial Secretary to the Birmingham and Western Branch of the Union, from which retired in 1927. In 1897 and 1898 he was President of the Birmingham Trades Council and also executive member of the Federation of General Workers.'

Apart from his trade union activity, Henry was a member of the Aston Board of Guardians from 1901-1910 and in 1911 was returned top of the poll for Washwood Heath Ward in the council elections. Henry went on to serve on the Tramways and Omnibus Committee and the Lighting, Stables and Refuse Disposal Committee. In May 1920 he was made an Alderman of the City and in 1922 became a member of the Municipal Bank Committee. He died on July 5, 1937 and the funeral at Washwood Heath Methodist Church was packed with old colleagues.

along by the fervour. He and a few other brass worker activists pressed for a wage rise, but they realised that their success could be assured only with the support of a trade union.

On April 18, 1872, they called a great meeting at the Town Hall. It was a stirring sight. Thousands of men harked to the call and packed the building to back the appeal for the formation of a Birmingham Brass Workers Society. Elected unanimously as secretary, Davis went on to organise brass workers elsewhere in England, becoming the leader of the National Society of Amalgamated Brassworkers with its headquarters at 70 Lionel Street.

Will Thorne and William John Davis battled against misery and fought to raise the standard of life for workers. They influenced trade unionism nationally and they'd be proud to see another Brummie, Bill Jordan, now leading the international trade union movement.

Trade unionists marching along Paradise Street during a May Day Parade probably in the late 1950s.

A Hero of the Great War: Arthur Vickers VC

He was a proper old soldier and he knew his duty did Arthur Vickers of Brummagem. Born in a back house in Woodcock Street, Gosta Green in 1882, he'd gone to Dartmouth Street School and as a young chap he joined the Royal Warwickshire Regiment – just two days before the end of the Boer War. He'd served with the colours for six years and then come out in 1908. No-one could ever say that he hadn't done his bit for King and Country – but a bit wasn't enough for Arthur Vickers. He was one of those blokes who was always willing and able to push himself past the last mile and that's what he did in 1914.

As the Kaiser built up his armed forces and threw back his shoulders all set for a fight, the fright and fury of conflict once more took hold of Britain. And so soon as ever war was declared, Arthur Vickers was there. He packed up his job as a millwright's mate at Lucas's and re-enlisted with his old regiment so that he could stand up for England and his pals.

Mind you, if they'd have seen him the Germans would probably have dismissed him as a fighting man. At just 5'2" Arthur was a short chap, so much so that he was nicknamed 'Midge' or 'Midget'. In fact, in August 1914 he'd gone to six different recruiting offices before he found someone to accept him back in the army despite his small stature.

But it would have been a mistake to ignore the martial qualities of Arthur Vickers – just as it was an act of folly for the Kaiser himself to have sneered that the British Expeditionary Force was a 'contemptible little army' which he would sweep out of

A wonderful photo of Arthur Vickers wearing his medals and sat behind the illuminated address which was presented to him by the City of Birmingham. Thanks to Dave Vaux.

Arthur Vickers is here on the left at the front of the Drumhead Service in Sutton Park on July 28, 1944. After the service, Arthur laid the wreath at the Cenotaph.

Flanders and into the sea. The Germans did not overcome the British Expeditionary Force and soon they were to learn that short as he was, Arthur Vickers was a fighting man whom they would have to respect.

Nineteen fifteen was not a good year for the British forces on the Western Front. There was a shortage of men, guns and ammunition and our lads were used mainly in support of French strategy. In these circumstances, the British had suffered a number of tactical defeats. One of them was the Battle of Loos at which Arthur Vickers distinguished himself by his gallantry.

On the morning of September 25, 1915 the 15th (Scottish) Division went over the top, pulled forward courageously by the skirl of the bagpipes, whilst Irish soldiers bravely chased after a football which they had kicked before them. The lads of the 2nd Royal Warwicks were up there with them. Part of the 7th Division, the Warwicks valorously rushed from their trenches at half-past six in the morning. Battling through a terrible wave of fire, they reached the first German trenches at the Hulloch Quarries – but they found that the thick barbed wire which protected the enemy lines had not been cut as it should have been by the British bombardment which had preceded the assault.

A smashing snap of Arthur Vickers later in life at West Heath sanatorium where he died of TB in 1944. Thanks to Matthew Vickers and Joan Bassett, whose dad was Arthur's brother.

That's where Midge Vickers showed his grit and guts. He was one of only four men in his company who had been issued with heavy and cumbersome wire cutters. With his mates falling all around him, Arthur took matters into his own hands. Instead of lying down to try and cut the wire and so give himself some protection, Arthur stood up to allow himself more leverage.

It was broad daylight and he was within 50 yards of the Germans, but Arthur took no cotter of the mayhem and violence all about him. As he told his sister, Amy Atkins of Park Road, Aston, 'I had to use both my hands until there was no more use in them'. And did he use those hands well, for Arthur cut two paths through the thickets of barbed wire and enabled his battalion to pass through and capture the first and second lines of the German trenches. Unhappily, later that day the Warwicks had to pull back because they were exposed through the withdrawal of British troops on their flanks.

That midnight on September 25, the Second Royal Warwicks presented themselves for muster. There were no officers left to take their names and out of a total of 523 men who had gone out to battle that morning, only 140 could call out. The rest were dead, wounded or missing in action. The casualties would have been even higher without the valiance of Arthur Vickers.

For his defiant spirit and outstanding bravery, Arthur Vickers was awarded the Médaille Militaire by the French and the Victoria Cross by the British. He was the first of six men from the Royal Warwicks to receive this the highest of his own country's accolades. Two months later, Arthur was honoured by his own City.

Although unable to be present at the ceremony in Victoria Square at which Lieutenant James VC was also honoured, Arthur's courage was made plain by Alderman Neville Chamberlain, the Lord Mayor. Birmingham's first citizen declared that there can have been few acts which were finer than that performed by Lance-Corporal Vickers for 'in the face of almost certain death, he voluntarily went out in murderous shell and rifle-fire, and cut the barbed wire which was holding up his battalion'.

Arthur received his VC from King George at Buckingham Palace in March 1916 and after the war, he was one of 320 holders of the medal who dined with the Prince of Wales (later the Duke of Windsor) in the Royal Gallery of the House of Lords on Armistice Day 1929. During peace time, Arthur served with the Territorials and worked at the GEC at Witton. Sadly, he died of TB in 1944 and fittingly his widow gave his medals to the museum of the Royal Warwicks.

In 1998, developers IM Properties erected a plaque in Arthur's honour at the Junction Six Industrial Park – the site of the old GEC factory – and recently his nephew and niece, Matthew Vickers and Joan Bassett, placed a wreath at their uncle's new headstone at Witton Cemetery. Is it not fitting that we should do more than that? Should not Arthur and all of Birmingham's VCs be honoured by their city with a civic memorial?

Chapter 3:

The Old End

Beyond the Edge of the World: Billesley

It was a strange feeling, leaving the old end to go beyond the edge of the known world – because that's what the junction of the Yardley Wood Road and Wake Green Road seemed like. Sometimes they had indeed ventured just past that boundary into the Dell and Swanshurst Park, and occasionally on a summer's evening they'd sat outside the 'Billesley' while their dad had drunk a couple a halves. But to be told that they were going to live further out than the pub and in the country was a startling thing.

They'd talked about it for weeks with their pals, yet they didn't really think that it was going to happen. Even on the day when they were supposed to be leaving, they never fully believed it until the arrival of the removal van, pulled by a pair of big, strong horses. Then they knew that this was serious. They must be going way out, else their old man would've got a hand cart from down The Lane. As their belongings were lugged on to the wagon, a few of the neighbours gathered about to say their taras. One of them whispered out loud to everyone in particular: 'They'll soon be back. They wunt like it out there in Billesley. It's in the middle of nowhere. They'll be cold and lonely and they'll soon come um. You mark my words.'

Despite her warnings, the little 'uns seemed dead happy at the prospect of living in a tree-scattered playground, although the older ones were subdued at the thought of leaving their mates. The old mon was a bit quiet as well, probably wondering at how the cribbage team down at the local would get on without him, but as for the mom – well, she was dead chuffed. For days she'd been telling them that they'd soon be having a front garden, a bath inside the house – not something stuck on the wall in the yard – plenty of hot water, their own toilet and good-sized kitchen. There was no doubt about it, she couldn't wait to get into their new council house.

Mind you, the whole lot of them became almost as excited as she was when they reached Brook Lane and saw all the building work going on. It was exhilarating to look at the houses in various stages of completion and to see how the council estate was marching all conqueringly across the fields. They felt almost like explorers setting off for a new land. Everything in Billesley was the best in the world Nowhere else had air as fresh. Nowhere else had fields so green. And nowhere else had birds that sung so sweetly.

It didn't matter that the kids had to traipse all the way to school at Dennis Road, Sparkbrook and Colmore Road, Kings Heath until Billesley School was opened in Trittiford Road in 1925. It didn't even matter that the rents were higher and that there were hardly any shops. What mattered was that they'd got a decent house in wonderful surroundings.

A most unusual shot of building work in Chinnbrook Road, Billesley in 1926. Thanks to Victor Pugh. Considering how many municipal houses wee constructed during the inter-war years, it is rare to come across photographic evidence of this activity.

A lot of people have asked if my family is connected with the Chinn Brook. Our family legend declares that we were tenant farmers by the Chinn Brook in Kings Heath and that the brook is named after us. However, we didn't come to Kings Heath until the 1820s whereas the name Chinn Brook dates back at least 1,000 years to the Anglo-Saxon period. So I don't think that we gave our name to the brook!

Derek Birch's mom and dad moved into Beauchamp Road, Billesley in 1933 when he was one year old. The first thing Derek remembers is having a street party 'for the king's coronation, which included a large marquee erected on the green. I went to Billesley School in Trittiford Road, going through nursery, infants, juniors to senior classes. At this time we had only retired or very young teachers. Miss Gibbons was only 16, Miss Jameson was 17. It was said that we were very lucky because a new building just away down the road had a gym, woodworking room, cookery room (the latter a great favourite with the boys) and domestic rooms for the girls.'

Derek well recalls the Anderson Shelters that 'everybody had in their back gardens plus two communal shelters on Yardley Wood Road – one opposite Brigfield Crescent and the other one opposite the Municipal Bank. During this time of war we were rather lucky as only a few bombs fell on Billesley. One demolished 6 houses in Chinnbrook Road by Chells Grove and though rebuilt after the war are noticed by their different construction. Another killed three of Mr Tippin's horses in his field by Billesley Common. The bus depot was left empty during the nights and buses were parked down Yardley Wood Road as a precaution. On Billesley Common we had ack ack guns. They also grew wheat and potatoes on the other side. On Swanshurst Park they had a heavy gun and during air raids we had to put all the crockery on the floor as when they fired this gun the houses would shake. Later when the air raids topped they removed this gun and Italian POWs were kept there.'

Gwen Bishop was born in Chinnbrook Road and recalls that in their living room 'we had the old black leaded grate, which my mother was forever polishing so that it gleamed'. On Friday nights, the water was heated in a great, big copper 'which took up about one third of the space of the bathroom, which was downstairs'. This is Gwen's photo of the 1937 Coronation Celebrations in Chells Grove, off Chinnbrook Road. On the back row left to right are Mrs Apted, Mrs Langford, unknown, Mrs Griffin and Mrs Sturgess; whilst on the front row are Mrs Dowson and Ivy Taylor, 'my Mom. The lad with his beret on is I think Stanley Langford.'

In fact the Langfords were amongst the first families to move into Chinnbrook Road in 1925. S. E. Langford was three at the time and over the next five years the youngster watched the area develop from farmlands and countryside into the suburb it is now. After Haunch Lane, Yardley Wood Road was virtually a country lane with the brook crossing it about 200 yards past what was the 'Valley' public house. The bus service came quickly to the area, with the 13 running along Yardley Wood Road and the 18A going up Haunch Lane towards Northfield and they the Austin. Shops were built round Trittiford Road, at the far end of Chinnbrook Road 'and later quite a lot were built in Haunch Lane. Three shops and a Municipal Bank were built on Yardley Wood Road by Brigfield Road.'

Miss D. A. Neal moved into Chinnbrook Road with her mother and father in April 1926 and still has 'the slip of paper granting my parents their tenancy'. Indeed, she still lives in the same house. She well remembers S. E. Langford as 'he and his parents and eventually five brothers lived opposite to us... I also knew Stan Taylor who had a sister Audrey who lived further up the road. Other names too I recall. Eric Henshaw, Tommy and Win Sparkes, Joan Clatworthy, Dora Rooke and Irene Winter to name a few of the firsts, including another Dorothy Neal (no relation) but the same age as myself and in the same class at Billesley School. We were given A and B after our names to distinguish us. I think I am the only original dweller left but often wonder what has happened to the other "youngsters".'

Work on the Billesley Estates had begun in 1921, soon after the end of the First World War, and by 1926 between 15 and 20 families were moving into the neighbourhood each week. There were two distinct parts to the district: the development on Ivy House Farm, where Oakcroft Road, Effingham Road, Worley Grove and others emerged – and that on Billesley Farm, the buildings of which have survived between Wold Walk and Hopton Grove. This area was a great triangle bounded by Trittiford Road the Yardley Wood Road and Chinn Brook Road and included Bromwall Road, Colemeadow Road and groves like Picton and Sellbourne.

Yet if Billesley was one of the earliest council estates in Birmingham, still it boasts rural enclaves which strike back to when an Anglo-Saxon called Bill made a ley – a clearing – up above the Chinn Brook.

E. Harris has sent in this cracking shot of the Billesley Carnegie Old Boys Football Club. His grandfather, Bert Harris, was a keen supporter and is first on the left in the back row, whilst Ken Taylor is third from the left. Ken Taylor was born in Aston in 1918 and he and his family moved to Chinnbrook Road in 1925. He stresses how 'we kids thought it was wonderful, with a big field at the back and a brook at the bottom of the field and a farm with animals on the other side. All our young years were taken up kicking balls and chasing each other. We had to walk to Colmore Rd School as Billesley School was not finished. At the age of 18 I played football for Billesley Carnegie Old Boys until I was called up for military service in June 1939, serving at Dunkirk, the Desert and Anzio beachhead. I did not return to Chinnbrook again because I got married on embarkation leave in 1942, I will never forget those happy days at Chinnbrook Rd.'

During the 1930s Margaret Holloway belonged to the Billesley Arcadian Band run by Mr and Mrs Bentley from School Road, Yardley Wood. The uniforms were blue, yellow and gold with white pumps and white socks.

Geoff Smith's parents, Albert and Lucy Smith were the caretakers at Trittiford Road School from 1935 until 1956. He notes that the housing development in Trittiford Road, between Bromwall Road and Trittiford Road, came after 1935 'as I can recall the houses being built, together with the "New School" as it became known which was an extension of the Trittiford Road School – although some 300 yards away from the main buildings. The "New School" included a science lab, a manual department where mainly woodwork teaching was intended, but the war intervened and we lads had to be content with cookery lessons in one of the two domestic science rooms. Pride of the "New School" was the gymnasium which was undoubtedly the best in Birmingham at the time. Later a kitchen was built on part of the garden where free meals were cooked and given to some of the not so well off kids.'

Glebe Land to Working-Class Heartland: The Bishopsgate Street Neighbourhood

Standing outside the Hall of Memory at the top end of Broad Street, harking at the cacophony of noises from all the people and vehicles shifting about and trying in vain to catch hold of the swirl of movement all around, it's hard to imagine that in the 1750s there was no Broad Street. Instead there was just a country path which led from Bewdley Street (now Victoria Square) and Swinford Street (the top end of New Street) to Five Ways and hence to Stourbridge and Bewdley.

Within a few years, however, things began to change. The country lane nearest to Brum ran along a slope which was gentle and it was here on Easy Hill that a grand house was built by the renowned Brummagem printer, John Baskerville. Now the site of Baskerville House, it was the presence of the home of the celebrated producer of books that led to the widening of the track in front of his home.

Soon after, the rest of the path disappeared to be replaced by a broadened street which ran all the way to the border with Edgbaston, just past Five Ways. The emergence of this aptly-named Broad Street came about because of the development of the Islington Estate on property owned by Saint Martin's Church. Bounded to the south by Islington Row and Bath Row and to the north west by Islington – now the Five Ways end of Broad Street – this glebe land, as it was known, was part of the living of the vicar and provided him with income. All Church of England parishes had such properties which could be farmed directly or leased out.

In the case of Saint Martin's, the development of this part of its glebe was allowed by an act of Parliament passed in 1773. Known as the Six Closes, or 'by ancient description called the Five Ways Closes', it consisted of upwards of 22 acres of land. Within fifteen years of the legislation, advertisements for building leases were advertised for the area and according to Pye's map of 1795 a number of streets were laid out.

Two of them ran downhill from Islington to Bath Row. These were the unsurprisingly-named Saint Martin's Street and the equally religious-sounding Bishopsgate Street. Going across them at a diagonal from Islington Row were William Street and Tennant Street. These recalled a William Tennant who had the advowson of Saint Martin's – that is, he had the right to appoint the vicar. For hundreds of years, this right had belonged to the lords of the manor, but it passed out of their hands in 1720 and it seems that William Tennant was patron of Saint Martin's for at least 50 years from 1771.

Building along the streets was slow and seems to have been held up by the long French Wars. However, development picked up with the coming of peace after the Battle of Waterloo in 1815, although William Street and Tennant Street still ran only just past Bishopsgate Street. Between there and Gas Street, there were small gardens through which ran two paths which would become Berkley Street and Holliday Street

An evocative photo of Bishopsgate Street at the turn of the twentieth century.

Les Pearson dad's family all lived nearby in Holliday Street, in the second house from the Corporation Yard at the side of Chequer's Walk. The first house was empty but had an old tramp dossing in it, and 'my Grandma's front door was up the entry, leading to the wash house in the middle of the yard'. Les's granddad was a very big man with a walrus moustache, flat cap, white muffler, very big boots and big buckled belt and 'my grandma was lovely having grey hair, glasses and always wore a wrap-around pinny and over that a flowered apron'.

When Les was old enough, his mom would give him thrupence for his tram fare from Tyseley to town so that he could fetch his dad's wages. His father worked close to Holliday Street, for BOC in Berkley Street and 'I would sit and wait in the warm canteen drinking a mug of tea, till my Dad came in with his money. I liked doing it because many of the men gave me a farthing to fetch some nicies. I loved it around there because we would go up to the Grenville Arms to feed the sheep they kept in the yard.'

Jean Smith was born at the top end of Bishopsgate Street at 2 back of 62 and lived there until her family moved to the bottom of the entry. She stayed there until she was sixteen and left home to live with her grandparents. There were a number of factories in the street, including SKF Ball Bearings, Hanger Motor Company, Cottam and Preedy, Cauls, Monks and Edmunds – where they made handbags, purses and other metal goods. And there was also Monks, at which were manufactured metal window frames and suchlike. In addition there were lots of little huckster's shops such as Camplings, 'on the corner of Tennant Street and for whom I used to run many miles per week backwards and forwards to Ward's pork butchers on Broad Street. I was given two caramels each time I went. It was worth it for me because I had always run out of sweet coupons.'

These back-to-back houses at 75-79, Tennant Street, leading to the corner with Stoke Street, are being renovated by the council during the 1950s. During these years, tens of thousands of people were on the waiting list for council properties and so as well as building new houses, maisonettes and flats, the corporation also had to improve many back-to-backs as a stop-gap measure.

Jane Taylor, nee Phipps, lived in one of these houses. Born at 4 back of 18, Stoke Street she moved to 77, Tennant Street when she was about ten

years old. In later years her sister's family, the Jonses's, lived next door at 76 and on the other side was Mr Davies and his family. Next door to them was June's aunt and uncle, the Hemmings. At the back of the house was a big yard 'and we had a bomb drop in the middle and the "Evening Despatch" took a picture with us all standing around and it was printed on 6th December 1940'. Across the way was where they delivered the pigs to Ward's the pork butcher's of Broad Street, while round the corner in Stoke Street lived Sid Moseley. He went about the streets selling his wares on a hand cart or a horse and cart. Sid wore a white coat and trilby hat and 'sometimes he would have a cartful of fresh peas and shout "fourpence a peck of peas!" or "tanner a pound strawberries or cherries" and would scoop them up with a saucer.'

Dr Wallace Hall tells me that his father ran a brass foundry at 166, Tennant Street for about 50 years. Mr Hall senior was born in 1892, the second of five brothers all of whom became brass founders and thus were the fourth generation of the family to work in the trade. After attending the Technical School in Suffolk Street, Mr Hall went to work and during the First World War he made brass ingots for rolling into sheet for the manufacture of cartridges.

By 1918 he was a foreman at Daniel and Arter in Highgate Street, but within a year he and his brothers decided to set up their own foundry in Tennant Street. The business had been run by A. E. Farmer, but now it operated as Hall Brothers and specialised in high quality castings such as memorial tablets and signs – including those for Sun Insurance in Bennetts Hill and for the 'Dolphin' pub in Acocks Green. In the 1930s, the brothers and their workers also made marine castings in nickel silver (silver bronze) for the Cunard liners the Queen Mary and Queen Elizabeth.

After the Second World War, it became difficult to find apprentices to work with the casters and planning legislation ensured that the foundry could not be expanded in Tennant Street. Hall's diversified into making diecasting in other premises but kept the sand foundry ticking over until the retirement of Bert and Jack New and Albert Cable – three cracking workers who'd been with the firm for 50 years. The lease to the premises was then surrendered to the freeholders and the premises were soon knocked down. As Wallace makes plain, 'so ended another of Brum's traditional businesses which produced craftsmanship of the highest quality, making fittings that are still in service in prestigious situations in this country and overseas'.

What a cracking shot of the 'Kings Arms' pubs on the corner of William Street and Bishopsgate Street in the late 1960s. When I put this photo in the **Evening Mail**, Mrs F. Timms recognised her late husband standing in the doorway. He was the licensee of the premises and his wife has 'some very happy memories of the years we spent there'.

Nora Oates nee Duggins was born at one back of 122 Bishopsgate Street. She recalls that there used to be a pigsty towards the bottom of the street, nearest to Granville Street, 'and the squeals when they were slaughtered were unbearable, also the blood that ran down the gutter was horrible to see. We used to buy a pig's bladder for a penny.' Opposite the home of the Duggins family was a bus depot and 'we used to wait outside for when the drivers was coming out because they gave us their lunch that they hadn't eaten. It was great we thought. Sometimes it was cheese or ham or porkpie, you see Carl in them days it was just plain food, you know like porridge or a piece of lard with salt on. We only had a saucer of tea right uptil I was 14 years of age . . . in bed at seven o'clock, up early the next morning to get the ashes up in the grate. My dad sold firewood for a living and when we were old enough we used to take the barrow to the place where they sold the wood in Oozells Street.'

George Fair was born in William Street in January 1923 and went to Tennant Street School until he was eleven and then to Pigot Street School. As a youngster he did a paper round for Charlie Shaw who had a shop in Tennant Street by Islington Row. Old Charlie only had one arm and used to have a pitch in the morning in Edmund Street by the Art Gallery, having a wicker basket to hold his papers in. George himself did his morning round in Tennant Street, Saint Martin's Street, Bishopsgate Street, Stoke Street and William Street -with a couple of deliveries in Holliday Street and Granville Street.

Of a night, George did Calthorpe Road, Harborne Road and Hagley Road as far as Lightwoods Park; whilst on a Sunday he delivered around the University of Birmingham 'till 12-00 then walked to the Ivy Bush on the Hagley Road and collected the wicker basket where Charlie used to sell papers. For all this I got 2/6per week. In those days I thought it was a fortune but my Mom used to have it because there was 6 of us at home in a 2 up 1 down and I had any tips myself.'

– named after William Holliday, a prominent businessman and mayor of Birmingham in 1863-4.

Both these streets were apparent by the later 1850s, as were Stoke Street, Granville Street and the curiously-shaped Communication Row, which snaked its way from Bath Row to William Street. Through their emergence, these streets destroyed the small gardens locally and, in 1876, an extension of the Midland Railway line went across the Jewish Cemetery in Granville Street. The faint remains of another Jewish Cemetery can be seen still, close to what was Betholom Row – Beth Olom being the Hebrew for the City of the Dead. This tiny cut through went between Bath Row and Islington Row and was also to have been cleared for the railway. However, after protestations from Jewish Brummies the line was deviated.

Although known officially as the Islington Estate, the district was seen by many as part of Ladywood. In fact it was a neighbourhood in its own right. From Granville Street westwards, it was covered mostly by back-to-back houses and it boasted its own shops, pubs and businesses. The buildings and their people were swept away in Brum's post-war redevelopments. As the area is now pulled into the orbit of the Broad Street's leisure-based activities, little remains to call out to us of the lives of those Brummies who made this a close-knit and hard-working neighbourhood.

From Fields to Streets: Farm Street, Hockley

Even as a young child, he always wondered why Farm Street was so-called. After all, there wasn't a farm anywhere in the street – long as it was – nor any real trace of rural Brum. In fact, the only open space in the whole of Hockley and Summer Lane was the Burbury Street Rec – and covered with asphalt, that was more of a playground than a park. Yet Farm Street it was, for all it was packed with badly built back-to-back houses, small shops, hidden-away workshops, and a handful of imposing public buildings. Like each of Brum's working-class streets, it was devoid of fresh air, greenery and trees. But although it could not boast the beauty of the country, still Farm Street had its attractions.

Striking eastwards from Hockley Hill, it ran parallel with the Hockley Brook until it met Summer Lane, one of Brum's oldest roads. By contrast, Farm Street emerged late in Brum's history, when development overwhelmed that triangle of land which would have as its points 'The Salutation' at the bottom of Snow Hill, the 'Benyon Arms' on Hockley Hill and the 'Woodman' on the corner of Asylum Road.

Owned by Miss Caroline Colmore, a descendant of a family which traced its origins deep into Brum's past, the area was covered by fields until the early 1800s. By then, only Barr Street, Smith Street, Hockley Street, Harford Street, Bond Street, Hampton Street and the bottom of Hospital Street had appeared – and Great Hampton Row remained a country lane going to Colmore Lodge, close to what would become the junction with Bridge Street West. The rural feel was enhanced by Hunter's Nursery which lay just across the Hockley Brook, but by the 1830s the district's look was changed drastically.

The catalyst was the cutting of New John Street West, and soon all the land to the south began to be built upon. A decade later, the making of Bridge Street West and Farm Street completed the process of urbanisation locally. With an expanding population and with growing numbers in the smaller street coming off it, Farm Street soon had its own church. Erected on the corner of Wheeler Street, St Matthias's was consecrated in 1855. Built in brick, it had a chancel, nave, aisles and north and south chapels, and a year later it became the centre of a new parish carved out of that of St George. It never celebrated its centenary, for in 1948 it was shut.

St Matthias had its schools in Wheeler Street, but the schools of St Saviour's in Bridge Street West were actually in Farm Street. They were opened as early as 1849, when they comprised only a school room, classroom and teacher's house, and they were closed in 1874. The church was not the only major building on Farm Street. There was also the Friends' Hall, which was opened in 1894 for use as an adult schoolroom, meeting place and coffee tavern. And then there was Farm Street School. Completed in 1873 for the Birmingham School Board, it could accommodate 1,055 pupils. Children then were charged fees ranging from 1d to 3d, but it is obvious that there was a lot of hardship for over one half of the pupils were exempt from any payment. Farm Street School was closed in 1941, and part of it was used as a civic restaurant before it re-opened as a junior and infant school in 1949.

A cracking shot of the 'White Swan' on the corner of Farm Street and Villa Street in the 1950s. Thanks to Professor Hans Reichenfeld whose father was for many years the well-respected doctor at the Birmingham Provident Dispensary which was on the opposite corner.

Len Baron's mom's family came from Farm Street and her two brothers lived at number 62. They were Tom and Charles Colin. Tom was 'well known and respected in the district for he worked as a parks policeman (park keeper) at Handsworth Park – a post that he obtained after he was demobbed', whilst Charley and another sister, Mary, 'were equally popular with their friends and neighbours in Farm Street'. Unfortunately, Charley was gassed during the war 'which no doubt caused his early death on the 19th December 1927'. His brother, Tom, died in 1938 aged 62. When Len, his bother and mother 'arrived to attend this funeral we found Farm Street packed with people who had gathered to pay their respects so we had much difficulty as I remember in reaching the house. It was a sad day for all concerned.' Len will always remember Farm Street with 'delight, respect and sorrow'.

Caroline Perryman only has to smell candles burning and it brings to mind her grandparents' house at 194, Farm Street – three doors from Summer Lane. Why? Well it was candles that lit up the gloom of the cellar in which the family slept during the Blitz on Brum in the Second World War. Tragically, Caroline lost her uncle Leonard in one air raid. An incendiary bomb had dropped in the yard of the 'Birmingham Arms' across the way and eighteen-year old Leonard went with others with buckets of sand to put out any fires. Terribly, the bomb went off and they were all killed. After scouring the mortuaries looking for him, Leonard's brother and dad found him – but were able to recognise him only by his signet ring.

Jessie Butler's memories are of Farm Street between 1930 and 1946 when she, her parents and her brothers attended the Friend's Hall for Sunday worship – three times each Sunday. First there was Sunday School from 3.00 p.m. to 4.00 p.m., then a there was a children's service for an hour from 6.00 p.m. and finally came the evening service at 7.30 p.m. There were also a number of weekly activities, including a dramatic society and young people's guild at which there were talks and discussions. For the more energetic there was a gymnasium and a dance on Saturdays. With other groups such as the Boys' and Girls' Brigades the intention was to help young people 'to grow up learning to be good citizens and to try and make our parents and Sunday School teachers proud of us'.

H. W. Rushton was in the Boy's Brigade connected to the Friends Hall and this photo shows their football team about 1949/1950. On the back row left to right are Len Cussold, Den Fisher, Peter Hampson, unknown, H. W. Rushton, George Edwards (ex Icknield Street and Aston Boys who 'made the back page of the Birmingham Gazette on Mondays at that time more than the G. Edwards of the Villa'), and Roy Gibbons. On the front row from the left are unknown, Tommy Reeves, Graham Canning, Wally Phipps, Ronnie Stretch ('what a comic') and John Moorhouse.

June Humphries well remembers Farm Street as she lived nearby in Bridge Street West and went to Saint Matthias's School on the corner of Wheeler Street and Farm Street. Her friends Grace and Lily Makepeace lived a few houses up from the school and on the corner opposite was Chaplin's the greengrocer where 'I bought many a specked apple and we used to ask for fruit for rabbits. The rabbit was me, of course, and we'd go munching into school – making sure the teacher didn't see us.' Then there was Charlie Bull, the butcher on the corner of Lennox Street and Farm Street 'where mom would send me for the pork bones for the stewpot to feed us kids. Further along was Burbury Street School where local dances were held at what was called the Burbo.

Opposite Charlie Bull's was a house recalled vividly by Mr R. Lawrence. On the corner of Great Russell Street and Farm Street, it was home to an Italian Brummie family called Polsenelli. Every Sunday afternoon they would sell ice cream from a huge galvanised drum which filled the hole in the front doorway: 'we kids would take the cups down and get them filled up for a few coppers. It was lovely ice cream and as you can imagine it was quickly sold out.' A few years later, the Polsenellis moved out and 'my wife's family moved in. My wife was just a young girl and they discovered that the kitchen floor had been laid with terrazzo in a magnificent fashion. Next door 'was a paper shop and when I was a kid every Sunday morning I had to fetch the Sunday paper and my dad's snuff'.

*Sarah Ward went to Burbury Street Junior and Infant School in Farm Street and after this was closed to become the Harry Lucas Comprehensive, she went to Farm Street Junior and Infant School. This photo is of Sarah 'when I was about three years old. It was taken by the **Evening Mail** as it was the first Lolly-Pop man in Birmingham, and it was on the corner of Farm Street and Burbury Street. The photographer arrived late and all the children had gone into the school so they asked if I could cross the road just for the photo. My mother is on the left.'*

Rachel Calder's father used to have a shop on the corner of Farm Street and Great King Street, Hockley. Originally, the premises were built as a public house and 'the story I heard was that the authorities would not grant a licence for this and that was the reason for the subsequent use as a shop. My grandmother came to Birmingham from Worcester in 1916 and rented the shop and living accommodation. The premises were extensive, covering three floors with cellars to which access could be obtained from inside the house, and from the rear yard by means of double lift-up doors (obviously made for the beer barrels).' The first tenant for the shop was Rachel's father, Joseph Sharpe – a Jewish chap from Poland who had fought in one of the Jewish units of the British Army during the First World War. When peace came, he became a naturalised citizen of the United Kingdom and anglicised his name.

Rachel's father was there until about 1924 when he emigrated to Australia and his brother, Samuel Skorupa, took over the shop. He turned it from ready-made to bespoke tailoring – a business which continued for many years. Samuel then moved to Handsworth to a workroom over a shop on the corner of Barker Street and Villa Road.' Rachel herself lived at the shop at 153, Great King Street from 1928 to 1936. Round the corner in Farm Street were several back-to-back houses and then came a rag and bone yard and Wither's Bakery. Across the way and also on the corner was Sprason's, next door to which was a cake shop that once had been a pawnshop. Nearby was a pub whose landlady was related to Sandy Powell, the well-known music hall comic.

Rachel's cousin was a member of a dance band and they used to practise in the room at the back of the shop, 'much to the annoyance of the people who lived in the houses in Farm Street as their premises were built right up against ours. After a short time into the practice sessions, we used to get a knock then the drummer would muffle his drum sticks and the brass players would mute their instruments and the pianist I think could only use the soft medal.' The band was known as 'The Veronians'.

As prominent were the local pubs. On the corner with Hospital Street was the 'Guildford Arms,' whilst on the north side of the street just along from Burbury Street and the Friends' Hall was the 'Fountain Inn'. Further up, on the corner with Villa Street, was the 'White Swan' and then on the corner of Hunters Vale came the 'Queen's Head'. Other notable businesses included Wathes, Cattell and Gurden, dairymen at numbers 385 to 388 near to which was Hodgson and Sons the funeral directors. Joining them were T. and W. Brough, the timber merchants, and Joseph Lucas with its scrapyard, canteen and receiving depot.

Like Joe Lucas, a poor kid who came out of Carver Street, Will Thorne was another Hockleyite who made his mark on the world. Born into poverty in Farm Street in October 1857, by the age of six he was out collaring in a rope factory. A hard grafter and strong thinker. Thorne was determined to improve the lot of his fellow workers and after he moved to London in the 1880s he founded the Gas Workers' Union and later became Labour MP for West Ham – a position he held for almost 40 years. Farm Street made him, as it did so many other Brummies.

Garrisons and Artillery: Garrison Lane

One of the most powerful images of the Victorian age was that of General Gordon and his small band of Egyptian soldiers defending Khartoum for ten desperate months against the forces of the Mahdi. Hungry and worn-out, their resistance was ended on January 26, 1885. He'd been offered safe passage from the besieged town, but Gordon didn't abandon his men. Dressed in a white uniform he strode down the steps of the local palace to face the victorious enemy and was killed by a spear thrust. Just two days away was a British relief force led by General Wolseley.

Gordon's death had a deep impact everywhere and in Birmingham it was commemorated in Gordon Street and Wolseley Street off Garrison Lane. In fact this neighbourhood can claim to be the most military-sounding in Brum, for it also boasts an Artillery Street, a Camp Street and a Garrison Street – whilst Barwell Road used to be called Castle Street.

A view of Garrison Lane in the 1950s, looking down the hill towards Birmingham's city centre.

Just six years old and living in Artillery Street, Gladys Farmer lost her dear mother in the terrible flu epidemic of 1918. Fortunately all her relatives lived locally. Her dad's mom looked after Gladys and her little sister, Lily while 'my dad's brothers and sisters were very kind to us'. Most importantly, 'my dear Dad took us with him everywhere he went. In the summer he played cricket and he looked lovely in white and his straw brimmer.' Both girls later went to Garrison Lane School and Gladys recalls Miss Thomson, Miss King and Miss Redstone amongst other teachers.

Gladys brings to mind many of the local people. Amongst them was Nurse Clements who 'never lost a baby. The saying was "have Nurse Clements you will be safe" and you had plenty of visits from her. There was a fruit shop in the late 20s and early 30s and you could have a carrot or swede, dates at a penny. If you missed the milkman you could go to a house in Garrison Lane and have a pennyworth in cups. Mr Baldwin pushed a cart around . . . and there was a very nice shop on the corner of Witton Street called Flint's. They were fruit and veg and were very good.' Then there was the corn shop in Garrison Lane – next door to which was a draper's shop; whilst in Wolseley Street a lady sold chitterlings, faggots and peas, pigs' feet and hodge, and in Artillery Street there was a family that made troach. Not forgetting, of course, the fish and chip shop of Harry Hawkins. Sadly Gladys died in 1998. She was a proper Brummie.

Photographs of Garrison Lane are rare. This one looks like it has been taken in the 1930s from the corner of Tilton Road, looking down at the distinctive Dutch-style flats known as 'The Mansions' that gathered in West, East, North and South Holmes. These buildings were constructed on an old clay pit – one of many in the vicinity. Notice the tram lines and then the youngster who is a shadow to the left of the first lamp post. This is because the cameras of the day could not capture people moving.

Brenda Ellis moved to Garrison Lane from Stroud in Gloucestershire, just before her marriage to Bob. She couldn't believe it when she came into the Ellis's yard because though it was very small it was a mass of flowers. The house was like a little palace inside and Bob's mom and dad made Brenda so welcome, while all the neighbours came round to see her: 'it was like being in another world but I immediately felt at home'. Now living in Atherstone, Brenda will never forget living in Garrison Lane where 'it was open house' and no doors were locked'.

Lilian Collier raises an intriguing question in my mind. She lived in Windsor Street and as the oldest of a big family used to take a bottle of tea and a piece of bread pudding and push the pram to Garrison Lane Rec so that the younger kids could play on the swings and roundabouts. But Lilian always knew the Rec as Itch-E-Cue Park. Is that where the 60's pop song came from?

Mrs D Hall's memories are of the lit tram coming down Garrison Lane, of hitting her knees against the lamp post when she swung round it on a rope, and when living in Templefield Street of her mom 'lugging the washing tub round the yard to the brewhouse'; whilst Mrs E Warwicker brings to mind her Aunt Polly and Uncle Arthur Sherlock's shop with an 'old Pop Jar on the counter with the big glass ball floating around.'

The connection with the armed forces stems from Garrison Farm, once on the high ground above the River Rea at the pudding-bag end of Tilton Road. Mentioned on a map from 1725, it could be that soldiers were garrisoned there once. What we do know is that much of the nearby land was owned by the wealthy Digby family. They had a big house at Tilton-on-the-Hill in Leicestershire and one of them married a celebrated 17th century beauty, Venetia Stanley. Their influence is remembered in Tilton Road and Venetia Road.

Both were developed in the 1880s, along with Sydney Road, Gray Street, Maxstoke Street and Templefield Street – which had been part of the bowling green and tea gardens attached to the 'Wrexham' pub on the Coventry Road. At the same time Garrison Farm became a brick works, one of many in the Bordesley and Small Heath areas which supplied Brum's builders with our city 's distinctive red bricks.

The mostly back-to-back housing at the bottom end of Garrison Lane was much older. Here Saltley Street, Witton Street, Lower Dartmouth Street and Garrison Street had been cut out of small gardens in the 1820s and 1830s. Saltley Street disappeared between 1910 and 1912 when the council bought the land from the Lench's Trust and cleared it for the laying out of Callowfield Recreation Ground. With its bandstand and bowling green it later became Garrison Lane Rec.

Fifteen years later, Birmingham's first inter-war corporation flats arose on an old clay pit between Garrison Lane and the Blues Ground – 180 of them in three-storey blocks made distinctive by their Dutch style roofs. Known by some as the Mansions, each flat had a bathroom and cost 8s 1d a week in rent. Other notable buildings remain in Garrison Lane. Up on the corner of Gray Street stands the 'Sportsman Inn' with its eye-catching tower which looks as if it's come out of the Middle Ages. Then close to Witton Street is Garrison Lane School, in use from 1873 and today a centre for community projects. Towards Bordesley Green is Tilton Road School opened in 1891. Closed in recent years it fell into disrepair, although it's being restored.

For all their importance, perhaps most the most significant building locally was the Universe Works in Garrison Lane. It took up almost the whole of the north side of the street – from Lawley Street to Midland Street. Owned by the Wright family, ropes were made on the premises. In particular the works was renowned for its combination of hemp and wire to make a rope that was strong, pliable and not easily corroded. No wonder Wright's was called upon to make the rope for the transatlantic cable connecting Britain with America in 1866.

Garrison Lane itself had many well known concerns, like Newton, Shakespeare and Company the sheet metal workers; Tommy Allen, the scrap metal merchant; Worral's, the lacquer manufacturers; Sheppard, Pettigrew and Company the brass cock founders; and Harry Major Lowe, the timber merchant. Then there were shopkeepers such as Raggy Rowley the wardrobe dealer, Henry Hawkins the fish and chip shop owner, John Smith the butcher, Eliza Willis the draper, Bill Power the coffee-house keeper,

Abel Calvert the outdoor man, Hunt's the greengrocer; and Henry Mitchell with his trio of shops near to Sydney Road.

Much of Garrison Lane was knocked down in the 1960s and recently some of it's been redeveloped as a part of the award-winning Bordesley Village. Yet none should forget Garrison Lane's significance as one of Old Brum's working-class heartlands.

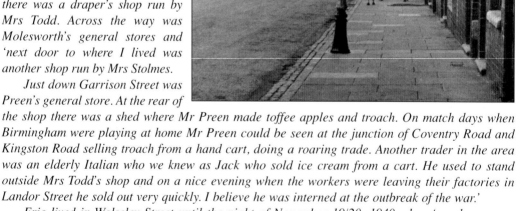

A smashing shot of kids in Tilton Road in the 1950s, looking down from Cattell Road and across Garrison Lane. It looks like it could be dinner time, with youngsters going to and from Tilton Road School across the way and on the right. The 'Royal George' pub is on the left, below Osborne, Tintern, Clifton, Stanley, Marrieon, Florence and Scott Places.

Eric Bailey was born in 1930 in Wolseley Street which was just around the corner from the Rookery, a terrace of back-to-backs in Garrison Street. His grandparents kept the shop at the corner of the yard in the Rookery and he remembers that on one corner of Garrison Street and Wolseley Street there was a draper's shop run by Mrs Todd. Across the way was Molesworth's general stores and 'next door to where I lived was another shop run by Mrs Stolmes.

Just down Garrison Street was Preen's general store. At the rear of the shop there was a shed where Mr Preen made toffee apples and troach. On match days when Birmingham were playing at home Mr Preen could be seen at the junction of Coventry Road and Kingston Road selling troach from a hand cart, doing a roaring trade. Another trader in the area was an elderly Italian who we knew as Jack who sold ice cream from a cart. He used to stand outside Mrs Todd's shop and on a nice evening when the workers were leaving their factories in Landor Street he sold out very quickly. I believe he was interned at the outbreak of the war.'

Eric lived in Wolseley Street until the night of November 19/20, 1940 when 'our house was badly damaged by a bomb which fell just outside the front. On this night, I understand from reports I have since read that more bombs were dropped on Birmingham than any other night and all around there were fires. The nearest fire was at Wright's Rope Works in Garrison Street. Fire pumps were drawing water from the canal at the top of the Rookery to fight the fires, also from the pools in the disused brick works referred to as the "Corns" by the locals. Some of the pools were of an unknown depth and resulted in many drowning tragedies particularly during the school holidays when children disregarded the warnings to keep away from the danger areas.'

A Clump of Rooks: Rookery Road, Handsworth

Was there once a clump of trees in Handsworth where nests of rooks were gathered so closely and totteringly that this rookery gave its name to a modern road? Perhaps there was, but whether or not rooks abounded in this part of Handsworth, certainly hereabouts there had been a large house called The Rookery.

It was not the only grand structure so called in the Birmingham area, for there is also a Rookery House in Erdington. A Georgian mansion, this was built by Abraham Spooner between 1725 and 1730 and it was set in pleasant parkland. Unlike its namesake, Rookery House, Handsworth is no more and less is known about it.

What is known is that it stood on the turnpike road to Wednesbury, today's Soho Road, and it was present by the later 1700s. In this period, Handsworth was still mostly rural – despite the presence of the Soho Works of Matthew Boulton. There were a number of farm such as Oxhill, Grove, Crick and Sycamore – which are recalled in road names – and here and there were the great homes of some of those who had made their wealth in Birmingham.

There were imposing structures like The Friary, Island House, New Inn Hall, Thornhill and Stockwell – all of which are brought to mind in modern roads – and, of course, The Rookery. The road which takes its name from the house was obvious by late eighteenth century, running from the turnpike up to Wilkes Green – the locality around today's junction of Antrobus and Albion Road – and up what is now Oxhill Road. This ran into Church Lane, which in itself went on to Hunts Green and the turnpike road to Walsall – now the junction of Wellington Road, Hamstead Road and Handsworth Wood Road.

Across the way from the bottom end of Rookery Road still stands the Old Town Hall at the fork of Slack Lane and College Road. Erected in the late 1400s, it has two crucks – curved timbers extending from the roof to the ground. The town hall is one of the finest examples in England of such a timber-framed. For generations it was owned by the Browne family, after whom is named, it is said, Brown's Green. This is that locality of Handsworth along the Handsworth Wood Road, close to World's End Road.

Although Handsworth was not a town until the later 1800s, the Old Town Hall was so named because it was here that the officers of Handsworth Parish were based. It was the residence of the constable, the overseer, the recruiting officer, the coroner's office, the workhouse master and the jailer, and often these posts were held by one and the same person. The building went through many owners until the Wilson family sold it to the City of Birmingham in 1938.

As the nineteenth century waxed, Handsworth was drawn increasingly within the orbit of Birmingham and builders took a fancy to it as a place ripe for development. It was close to the big city and it was expansive. However, the urbanisation of the district was long-drawn out and piecemeal. With regard to the Rookery Road neighbourhood, ,the area to the east as far as the Hamstead Road was mostly cut out with roads in the

A. F. Sowley has sent me this poignant photograph of the pre-Christmas dance at Rookery Road School in December 1939. Notice the blackout curtains draped over the windows behind the youngsters. In the ensuing years many of the lads in this photo went into the Army, Navy and Airforce and at least two joined the Royal Marines. To the best of Mr Sowley's knowledge one of those chaps was killed, whilst equally sadly, one of the girls was killed in a bomb that fell on Rookery Road.

Iris Welde attended Rookery Road School from 1930 to 1939 and remembers that in the senior school there was a brass plate in the centre of the floor which read 'On this spot stood Captain Scott'. On the walls 'were framed photographs of groups of men in what I now think were expedition clothes. They stated Scott of the Antarctica etc. but I do not recall what the captain said. I would very much like to know the connection Scott had with the school or was it some sort of memorial.'

Albert Davies went to live in Antrobus Road in 1925 when he was four years old and he explains that because Rookery Road was so long 'it was almost like three separate villages – Albert Road, with its own shops, Antrobus Road with its own shops and Oxhill Road with its own shops. The shops that were within Albert Road area were fairly high class. On the corner was a shop where they ground the coffee beans, unheard of at that time; also there was a shop called Caistries, a delicatessen, then a butcher's shop, and a shop where you could buy all the feed and hay for three horses that pulled the delivery cats.' At the back of this latter shop was a dairy and next door to the high-class grocer's was a Baines's bread and cake shop. On the other corner was Vernull's, the greengrocer and farther up was a shop that sold faggots and peas, tripe, chitterlings and such like.

Nora Hare was born in Warstone Terrace, which ran between Alfred Road and Rookery Road and in parallel with the Soho Road, in 1905 and as a child well recalls 'climbing on our garden wall which adjoined the grounds of a large house called "Eskdale" owned by two sisters named Jenkins who wanted to adopt me when I was 3 years old. There were very large old trees all round the grounds full of rooks nests which were there long before my time, but how long I do not know, but I know for certain that is how Rookery Road got its name.'

My mate, Laurie Hornsby, lived in Brunswick Gardens at the bottom of Antrobus Road and he tells me that after the Rookery Picture House closed it became the 'Plaza' Ballroom under the guidance of the well-known Mary and Joe Regan who also had the 'Ritz' in Kings Heath and the Old Hill Plaza. The Rookery Road venue was hugely popular and it featured world-class acts such as the 'Beatles' and the 'Rolling Stones'. Laurie stresses that 'you name them, they appeared there. The only big name they didn't have was Elvis Presley. Mind you, they did have Big Albert Chapman on the door – now best known through his ownership of 'The Elbow Room'. Sadly, the Plaza closed down in the late 1960s and became a carpet warehouse before becoming a temple.

1880s and 1890s. This large district was made a square by Church Lane to the north and the Soho Road to the south.

Meanwhile, the bell-shaped district to the west of Rookery Road was bounded by Oxhill, Sandwell and Holyhead Roads and was developed during the 1890s. In both localities, tunnel-back houses predominated. Built in long terraces in generally straight roads, they were at least three-bedroomed and boasted three rooms downstairs and their own lavatories washing facilities. Such homes were popular both with the upper working class and the lower middle class, although in the Rookery Road neighbourhood there prevailed a distinctly middle class feel.

The scene in Rookery Road after the air raid of June 27, 1942. This was the last big enemy attack on Brum of the war. At least 60 German planes dropped bombs that night and caused about 283 fires across the city. Rookery Road was devastated and tragically, a number of residents were killed. Amongst them were the mother and older sister of Midge Maidden. They had paused to collect blankets for Midge and her brother and sister and Elsie Maiden's last thoughts and actions were to serve us'. Others who died were the some of the Priestmans and Bonds. May they rest in peace.

Philip Cotterell was born in Grafton Road but when he was one he was moved to Rookery Road where his mom and dad had a grocery shop. His family told him about the raid in 1942 in which the shop was demolished and of how 'my Grandma had a feeling something was going to happen that night so she wanted to down the air raid shelter'. As Philip's dad opened the door of the shelter there was an explosion in the sky at which 'he looked up and said that is by the shop. He said, "I must get down there", which he did and found complete devastation. The man who normally stood by my grandfather who was firewatching was killed.'

Geoffrey Thomas is the lad wearing the top hat and moustache who is in the centre of the third row from the bottom. His sister, Jean, has given me this photo which was taken at a children's party at the 'Farcroft Hotel' that was given by the manager, Jimmy Murphy, on the occasion of the birthday of his daughter, Peggy. Many people have written to say that Jimmy was a gentleman and that he was a very popular landlord. From Ireland, he had connections with various boxers and men like Jack Hood and Jack Petersen would visit the pub's bowling green – which was the first in the Birmingham area to be floodlit. Jean also states that her father had a wholesale provision merchant's business in Rookery Road, opposite the 'Farcroft'. She herself was born in Rookery Road and went to Rookery Road School for four years. Barbara Smith couldn't believe her eyes when she studied this photo in the Evening Mail *'for there was my Mom and two of my uncles. My grandfather was big pals with Jim Murphy and I remember meeting him often as a child'.*

Alfred J. Smith was born in Rookery Road in March 1917, in a block of six little cottages. These were terraced houses with no gas or electricity and no running water. Each pair of the cottages shared a common brew-house and toilet across a yard that was open to all the houses and 'where we all hung washing to dry'. Mrs Morris's shop did a good trade in paraffin 'for the old lamps that we all had and all cooking was done on a coal fire with hobs and a small oven adjoining, winter and summer alike'.

Alfred was the middle one of a family of five children who all went to Rookery Road School. A few doors up lived Sidney Lucas who became a director of West Bromwich Albion and Alfred also recalls the building of the 'Farcroft Hotel' in the 1920s 'and the men measuring the road with those chairs ready for the start of the Outer Circle bus route. The very first buses were second-hand red ones bought from London and had solid tyres. When they trundled down Rookery Road, my father said they were gradually loosening the foundations of our cottage.'

Despite the rapid emergence of housing at the end of the nineteenth century, open land abounded until the inter-war years. Oxhill Farm could be found between Astley Road and Aylesford Road and between this last and Newcombe Road was a cricket ground – through which Mervyn Road now runs.

There was another large space between Albion Road and Hamilton Road, – as there was between this latter and the big houses remaining on the Holyhead Road. This is now Oaklands Sports and Social School. And east of Rookery Road towards Grove Lane, allotments and cricket grounds dominated the area – where there is now a development of 1930s houses.

The rapid growth of population in the Rookery Road neighbourhood in 1898 led to the opening of schools between Laurel Road and Mount Pleasant. Built and maintained by Handsworth School Board, they were operated by Birmingham after Handsworth became part of the city in 1911.

Just before the outbreak of the First World, in April 1914, the Rookery Picture Palace was opened by G. F. McDonald. It closed down in 1957 and is now a temple. Since the 1950s, this part of Handsworth has become a multi-cultural area in which people of all races live side by side. Indeed, it is probably one of the most diverse neighbourhoods in Britain and holds out a beacon as to how we can all learn to live together.

The Hills are Alive: Sparkhill

With 32 miles of cuts, we've got more canals than Venice. With our magnificent recreation grounds, we've got more parks than Paris. And though we're not celebrated for our steep slopes, we've got more hills than Rome! Just think of them all. There's Bennetts Hill, Snow Hill, Constitution Hill, Ludgate Hill, Newhall Hill, Key Hill, Singer's Hill and Camp Hill – and that's just around the city centre. To the west of Brum there's Summer Hill, Spring Hill, Hockley Hill and Soho Hill. On the north side there's Hamstead Hill, Tower Hill, Gravelly Hill, Beacon Hill, Potter's Hill in Aston, Marsh Hill in Stockland Green and Holborn Hill in Nechells. Finally, to the south-west there's Parson's Hill in Kings Norton, Cannon Hill and Park Hill in Moseley, while on the south east there's Kingston Hill in Bordesley, Alum Rock's Shaw Hill, Red Hill in Hay Mills and Tyseley Hill

And of course, there's Sparkhill – a bank which takes its name from a stream. The Spark Brook rises in Belle Walk, Moseley and although in 1511 an over-enthusiastic observer exclaimed it was a 'torrent' it's not really much of a flow. Shallow and short, it moves down Yardley Wood Road and Stoney Lane before turning sharply into Highgate Road. From there it goes over the Stratford Road and along Walford Road until it joins the River Cole at the Ackers, by the old BSA sports ground. Although now mostly culverted and hidden underground, the Spark's course is still shadowed by the hill which shares its name.

For centuries Sparkhill was a quiet, rural spot. In the Middle Ages it was farmed by the Sparke family and as late as the 1890s much of the district was agricultural. The rural feel was emphasised by places like Holly Cottage, Hazeldell, Spark Hill Villa and Lyra Cottage – as well as by roads such as Teddy's Lane (now Court Road) and Jenny's Lane (today part of Baker Street). Such spots were overwhelmed by the outpouring of Brum. This transformation started in the late 1850s when the land between the Warwick and Stratford Roads was taken over by a building society which parcelled out the estate amongst its working–class members. In this way, each of them became property owners and gained the right vote. A number of short streets were made, including one named after Joseph Sturge, a Birmingham manufacturer who wanted the vote extended to all working-class men. Now called St John's Road, Stratford and Shakespeare Streets. This quarter was like a village. It had its own pub, the 'Cherry Arbour', and because it was developed in a piecemeal way its houses were different styles.

Nearby, another small, tight-knit neighbourhood soon grew up around Mountford Street and Lea Road, but from the late 1880s the rest of Sparkhill was built over in a more precise manner. Between Walford and Warwick Roads, and between St John's and Formans Roads, the new streets were straighter, longer and lined with terraces of three-up three-down tunnel backs, each with its own back garden, coalhouse and lavatory. However, in the triangular plot formed by Durham Road, Stoney Lane and Alfred Road there were larger houses, often with an attic, for the lower middle class.

The top of Sparkhill, looking down towards the junction of Durham Road and Saint John's Road from the bottom of Showell Green Lane, in the early 1900s. The house and shops on the right are just along from Castleford Road.

Betsy Blundell (nee Amott) recollects that Pat Collins held one of his fairs in Sparkhill in 1925 in Walford Road. Five years later 'they held what was called the Greatest Show in Birmingham and, at a Valentine's Day dance, they put on mock marriages over the anvil which they were told had come from Gretna Green. The blacksmith there was from Scotland as well and some couples went through these "mock marriages". Then the trouble broke out because some of the girls thought they were really married, the Church kicked up a fuss and that was the end of the matter – but it caused a lot of trouble at the time!'

Joan Coates was born in Percy Road, Sparkhill in 1926. Half of the road was in Greet and the other half was in Sparkhill – 'Greet is Warwick Road end and Sparkhill is Formans Road end. They were mostly back-to-backs in Greet but we were fortunate to have an outside lavatory, coal house, miskin shed, a copper in the kitchen, and the bath hanging outside the kitchen on a hook on the wall. We also had quite a big garden. There was a small farm at the bottom of our gardens but it flooded one year from the river Cole and Farmer Jones ("Old Jonah") lost most of his animals. He bought another farm somewhere in Shirley but used the old pig sties by us for cooking his pig swill and Oh Boy! did it stink. We used to get over on the field and play until the farmer came and we've been chased off many times by his dog. We used to make a dam in the River Cole that we could swim. I often wondered if it was through us kids that his farm flooded. He sold up eventually to the factory in Percy Road (Wright, Bingley and Gill) and it was turned into a football pitch but was dug up during the war to make a huge static water tank for putting out fire bombs etc. There was a young boy drowned in it during the war.'

By the dawn of the twentieth century, Sparkhill was a district humming with activity – but it didn't become part of Brum until 1911. Before then it belonged to Yardley, Worcestershire, whose council house is now Sparkhill Library. Alongside it are other structures put up by the old county – a police station, a magistrate's court, a fire station and a public works depot. They're not the only noticeable buildings in the district. St John's Church, resplendent in its red brick and terracotta and stone dressings stands proudly at the top of Sparkhill.

Opened in 1889, it's close to the distinctive citadel of the Salvation Army, whilst close by in Evelyn Road is the impressive, Byzantine-type Catholic Church of the English Martyrs. Then there's the 'Piccadilly' Picture House, the old Sparkhill Commercial School and the 'Mermaid Inn', a pub since the 1600s and now splendidly refurbished as a balti restaurant.

A really evocative shot of the 'Mermaid' on the corner of the Warwick Road and the Stratford Road, Sparkhill in the late 1800s. Jack Rivett of Sparkhill has lived in the district all his life, recalling that he'd leave his home in Johnson Close after school to take Fowler's Dairies horses to the farrier in Baker Street. He's spent most of the last 50 years in St John's Road and mentions that his step father had a hansom cab-rank and stabled his horses at the back of the 'Mermaid' pub. Jack's entire family worked for the City Transport 'but I was a market trader. When I was a little lad I had to get up at 6am and push a truck from Sparkhill to Camp Hill to Harrison's the bakers. It was loaded with pikelets that my gran had made. I'd get 6d a week for this and spend it on 'specks' from Westwoods, a bottle of pop, the pictures – and I still had the money to buy my mom a bunch of flowers.'

Children enjoying themselves at the street party in Mountford Street, Sparkhill put on to celebrate the silver jubilee of George V and Queen Mary in 1935. This is one of the family photos of Jeanne Brown, whose family were a real Sparkhill crowd. Her mom, Doll Edkins, was brought up in Mountford Street, Sparkhill and went to Greet School nearby. She moved to Knowle Road after marrying Len Thomas and stayed there until she was 81. For many years, Doll and Len used to go to the Saturday night club in the upstairs room at the 'Cherry Arbour' in Shakespeare Street – where Jean actually met her husband, Barrie.

Shopping was something Jean loved, especially when her mom took her to the Co-op grocers at Springfield 'where they used to put the money in a metal tube which shot across the ceiling on wires to the office and it came back with the change in it.' Then there was Mannies where Jean and her friend would buy cheap wool and material 'and make ourselves blouses and knit cardigans during the school holidays when we were older. She had an old Singer hand machine and I had my Gran's old treadle one. We used to feel like the "Pig's Feet" when we got dressed up for youth club.'

Jeanne was a keen member of the 282nd Brownies and Guides at Sparkhill Congregational Church on the Stratford Road. On one occasion she and her mates wheeled around a little pram in which to collect jam jars. In total, they fetched in over 1,000 jam jars and also gathered in a load of old newspapers. As well as being in the Brownies, Jean was also in the youth club at the Congregational Church and 'we used to have great fun learning the Old Tyme dances like the Valeta, the St Bernard's Waltz, the Dashing White Sergeant, the Palais Glide and lots more to an old wind-up gramophone. We learnt to do square dancing as well and we used to go on Bank Holiday outings to the Lickey Hills, Clent and Shropshire.'

Up the hill and down to Showell Green Lane the Stratford Road was lined with retailers. There were no fewer than six bread shops – Highley's, Wright's, Baines's, Wimbush's (two) and Braggs, the only one left. There were big national names like Boot's Woolworth's, Timpson's and Dewhurst's, and there were outlets for most of Brum's own leading firms, such as Mason's the grocer, Foster Brother's the outfitter, Harris' the cleaner, Payne's the shoe repairer and Hayne's' the butcher who has just stopped trading.

There was also a host of smaller, specialist shopkeepers such as Anne Goldby's gowns, Moss Zissman – where I got my first suit – and Gould's the tailors, who's there today. Then there was that wonderland of an iron-monger's, Harry Essex and not far away Westwood's, the renowned greengrocer and fishmonger. Up the road was Bimbo's noted snack bar and across the main drag was one of the best cooked meat shops in Brummagem – Tabberner's. Can you remember their mouthwatering a la mode beef, their York ham, their pig's trotters, their home-made faggots? They may be gone but the taste still lingers.

Upper and Lower Villages: Stechford

Perhaps best known today for its police station and swimming baths on the Outer Circle 11 route, Stechford is one of Brum's districts which strikes deep into the Middle Ages. Hard on the boundary of Yardley in Worcestershire with both Little Bromwich and Castle Bromwich in Warwickshire, it is mentioned in 1275 as Sticheforde. Then, sometime in 1300 or 1301, a William of Berwode granted lands in Wodibromwis to Alice daughter of Adam Smith of Stichesford.

If we pronounce the 'ch' of Stichesforde as a 'k', the origins of the name become obvious. It was Stikesforde, a ford of sticks over the River Cole. In fact, the district remained known as Stichford until the mid-nineteenth century when the local railway station was mistakenly spelled as Stechford.

The hamlet of Sticheforde grew up on a gravel patch which was drier than the surrounding land of heavy clay and which allowed easy cultivation and an accessible supply of water from shallow wells. It was reached from Yardley Village by way of Flaxleye, now Flaxley Road, which was noted as early as 1327. One of the early inhabitants of the place was John atte Forde, who is mentioned in a deed from 1345 when he passed on lands to his son. His took his name from the place where he lived, at the ford. Across the River Cole and in Little Bromwich was Stechford Mill, which was in use from the later Middle Ages until the mid-1800s; whilst Stechford Hall lay in Castle Bromwich about where Beaufort Avenue now runs.

For all its individuality, Stechford was much nearer to the village of Yardley than were distant hamlets like Greet or isolated farmsteads such as Billesley. As a result, Stechford and Yardley were connected closely. Indeed Stycheforde Felde was one of the great open fields of the manor.

For centuries, Stechford remained a small settlement on the edge of Yardley, bounded by the River Cole to the north and west and by fields to the south and east. Distant as it was from the burgeoning Birmingham, its development was late and did not begin until after a suburban railway station was opened in 1844. Even then, urbanisation was slow, although by 1877 the growing population could worship at a Wesleyan chapel and at an iron mission church of Saint Edburgha's, Yardley. Becoming known as All Saints this structure on Alfred Road was replaced with a permanent building in 1892. Four years later, Stechford Infants School opened in Albert Road.

By this date Stechford had two villages. The upper village lay between Stechford junction and Victoria Road – although Albert Road and Lyttleton Road struck southwards to Yardley Fields Road and Fieldhouse Farm. Over the railway line was the lower village, where Northcote Road was apparent and nearby there were a few houses close to the 'Bull's Head'. To the east and along Flaxley Road was Fir Tree Farm, close to the junction of Flaxley Road, and the modern Old Farm Road was Hill House Farm; near to Church Lane and Flaxley Lane was Church End Farm; and just by Church Road and Yardley Fields Road was Church Road Farm.

By the First World War, more buildings had extended both the upper and lower villages and after the coming of peace in 1919, the great swathes of open land in Stechford mostly fell beneath housing. Church End Farm and Fir Tree Farm were taken over and developed as part of the Lea Hall Estate; whilst 600 houses were constructed on the Riddings Estate along with the Glebe Farm development. Although much of their land was also built upon during the 1920s and 1930s, Field House Farm, Hill House Farm and Church Road Farm all survived for a few years after 1945.

What a cracking shot of the 'Bull's Head', in the lower village of Stechford, some time in the early years of the twentieth centre. (Thanks to Bill Fox). It looks like there's a few breadmen who've popped in to Mr Waring's pub for a couple a three halves! There's a bread van belonging to Charles Waldron of 310, Bolton Road, Small Heath; another owned by the famed Harding's of Hay Mills and South Yardley; and one attached to Hovis. Notice the chicken in front of the horse on the right and the fact that the right-hand room of the pub is the Smoke Room. Stechford itself had its own celebrated baker, H. Holtom of Albert Road.

Elsie Truman, as was, spent many happy hours at the 'Stechford Methodist Youth Club' in Lyttleton Road, Stechford in the late 1940s and early 1950s. There were plenty of activities to get involved with, such as football, cricket, netball, table tennis and dramatics and 'we also went on charabanc trips which were great fun. Most of us belonged to the Boys' Brigade and Girls' Brigade so we were expected to attend church on Sundays, not many stayed away. We met two evenings a week and I know that many met their future partners there.'

Bill Drew and his sister have fond memories of Stechford. They lived in a back-to-back house in Aston but their dad had an allotment in Stechford 'and since we grew enough for our own needs, our neighbours had the benefit of cheap vegetables'. Peggy Sutton was actually born in Stechford in the 1930s and 'it was a lovely place to grow up. We lived in Redthorn Grove and used to play on the "Meadows" (where the baths are now) which were fronted by some prefabs. We belonged to the Methodist Church in Lyttleton Road, but most of my friends belonged to the Corpus Christi also in Lyttleton Road. Everyone knew each other. A lot of the men worked at either the Parkinson Cowan in Station Road or Levis (on the other side of Station Road). My Gran used to live by the station and we used to sit for hours in her lovely big back garden watching the trains go past.

Today, Stechford is marked out by the various stages of its development, but the old village centre continues as a focal point – if only for its memorial dedicated to the local men who died in the First World War.

This photo shows Val Preece standing with her dad in 1940/41 outside Stechford Railway Station. She is holding a tennis racquet and gas mask. In the background is Parkinson's factory, by which a stream that used to smell awfully as it went down to the River Cole. Val's family moved to Stechford in 1940 and she went to Albert Road School. About three months after starting 'we all had to take home a letter about evacuation. I had been away right at the beginning of the war to stay with an aunt in Wales but came home when nothing happened. However, the bombing began (presumably they were aiming for Parkinson's factory and Booth's factory Lea Hall), and I remember being tucked up under the stairs. We had the front window blown out twice and repaired. The third time Dad left it boarded up until near the end of the war. Mr Baldwin was the head of Albert Road and I have some fond memories of him. We had some excellent teachers – I remember Miss Tinsley, Miss Simcox, Miss Evans and Mrs Wheatley who taught needlework.'

From the age of six months, Kaye Downing lived with her parents in a council house in Manor Road. In those days the area 'was very rural, there were horses and cows in the fields adjoining the house garden'. At the top of the road was archway bridge, beyond which were hay farms, fields and a stud farm for horses which gave its name to Stud Lane'. Amongst the shops strong in Kaye's memory are a cobblers in a sort of shed building opposite the station; Joiner's the bakers; Baldwin's the ironmonger's; a newsagent; Lowe's the greengrocer's; Turner's who sold furniture; Aston's the butcher and 'the one I liked best, Bickley's, who sold dresses, hats, etc. I remember one hat I had, it was straw cloche with velvet bows on it and I'd admired it for ages before my mother bought it for me. On the opposite side of the road, facing where the baths are now, was another row of shops. Ellison, another butcher; a grocer's; Spooner's hairdressers; Billy Williams, coats, hats etc; and Holton's baby- wear and under-wear. Mrs Holton was the mother of Barbara my school friend. We are still friends to this day. Last but not least Nairn's run by a delightful Scottish lady. They sold confectionery at Easter, chocolate eggs, bunnies and chickens and at Christmas beautiful Christmas cake decorations in china.'

The Memorial to the men of Stechford who died in the Great War of 1914-1918, looking down towards Albert Road. This photo was taken in 1952.

Barbara Hill has lived in Stechford all her life and 'I remember all the shops we had. You could buy anything you wanted. there was one shop where you could buy prams, sewing machines, bikes, and children's toys at Christmas'. This was Case's and 'I remember that me and my friends used to run up to the butcher's when the cattle truck came to bring in the sheep and cows to be killed for the shop'. Then, on some Sunday mornings, there was the little old lady who would sing hymns in the middle of the road and 'Mom would give me a few coppers to give her and another lady would come some days in a pony and trap, selling milk and we used to buy a pint of milk off her'. Now and then, the circus would set up on land in Richmond Road, before the houses were built, and 'we used to watch the elephants come down the road and there was a farm cottage where the children's home is now'.

Seventy-six years ago and when he was eight, Mr Fenner's family moved from Aston to Treaford Hall in Treaford Lane. Mr Fenner senior was a showman and moved in with all his equipment – fairground rides, traction engines and the like. Four years later, the family bought Tomlinson's Farm in Stechford, 'a lovely spot alongside the River Cole'. In the summer time a fair was set up and in the winter the Fenners and other showmen pulled the fair down and turned it into a depot for fuel.

Land of the Bath Tub: West Heath

It is story worthy of a film, of how a firm which made ladies' compacts and hairpins in old Birmingham gave birth to a radio company which moved to the outskirts of the city at West Heath and made a significant contribution to the British war effort against Hitler's Germany. But it isn't a story of make believe. It's a true story and a thrilling one at that, filled as it is with inventiveness, determination, skill and valour.

The beginnings of the tale can be traced back to 1860 when a business called Jarrett and Rainsford was formed. Based in Islington, then an extension of Broad Street, it made pins which were sold wholesale and many of which were exported. By the early years of the twentieth century, the company had added hairpins to its list of products and was employing a remarkable man called George A. Laughton.

George was in charge of a small section of the firm which concentrated on coronation badges and flags. Some of the components were supplied by a little gaffer who was unreliable and so Laughton took the decision to buy him out. Because his wife was reading a novel in which the hero was called Stratton, he decided to take this name for that of the new company.

Continuing to work at Jarrett and Rainsford's, Laughton still found time to make a success of his own concern by turning out men's jewellery, ladies' compacts and a selection of small goods such as thimbles, knitting needles, hat pins and crochet hooks. Laughton's abilities obviously impressed his employers and in 1919 they bought Stratton and made him a partner in the expanded company.

The new business of Jarrett, Rainsford and Laughton had a number of premises in and about Kent Street, Gooch Street and Lower Essex Street. But soon it was beset by a disastrous fall in the sales of hairpins caused by the popularity of new, shorter hairstyles such as the bob and shingle. With a plant able to make six tons of hairpins a week, it was essential that something was done to keep people working. It was.

George Stratton Laughton, the eldest son of George A. Laughton, was a wireless enthusiast and he suggested that the machinery be turned to making radio components. His idea was taken up in 1923 when Stratton Communication Radio was founded. The trade name of Eddystone was chosen for the new wares because of the world famous lighthouse off Plymouth which exuded strength and reliability.

Located at the Balmoral Works in Bromsgrove Street, Stratton's soon came to be known not only as a manufacturer of components but also as a designer and maker of receivers. By 1927, it had focused on higher radio frequencies, which then were almost unused except in experimental transmissions. It was a far-sighted move, for the BBC and broadcasters in foreign countries soon introduced high frequency broadcasting. Stratton's itself produced a short-wave receiver which was the only set available commercially which was capable of the long-distance reception of the new BBC short wave services.

By now the firm had pulled out of the domestic market and was concentrating on commercial business. During the 1930s it developed portable VHF two-way equipment and following the Munich Crisis of 1938, when war with Germany looked likely, the Metropolitan Police ordered equipment for an automatic wireless telephone which would provide communication between all of the force's 95 stations. Stratton's also developed a differential condenser for use on high frequencies. This was incorporated in special 'Identification Friend or Foe' equipment carried by British aircraft and which allowed our airmen to react immediately and properly towards approaching aircraft.

Located as it was in central Birmingham, Stratton's was in midst of some of the most heavily-bombed districts in Britain and on the night of October 24, 1940, an oil bomb hit the Balmoral Works in Bromsgrove Street. A fierce fire blazed up and on

Assembling Eddystone Receivers in the former ladies dressing rooms at the Bath Tub, West Heath in 1941.

Alf Davies was born at 32, Lilley Lane, West Heath on September 16, 1914 and lived there until he married in 1940. He recalls that the trams stopped at Cotteridge, although some people felt that there was a tram shed by the 'Man in the Moon' pub. In fact, this was a farm until it was demolished and turned into a petrol station and garage owned by Patrick Motors. In those days, West Heath Road 'started as the Fordrough which then was a cart track which went through to Kings Norton past the Glass Works'. From when she was born in 1939 until December 1962, Carole C. Howell lived off the Redditch Road, close to the 'Man in the Moon' and remembers that the Redditch Road dual carriageway was started before the war but was abandoned when hostilities broke out. It was not completed for many years and Carole remembers picking blackberries there.

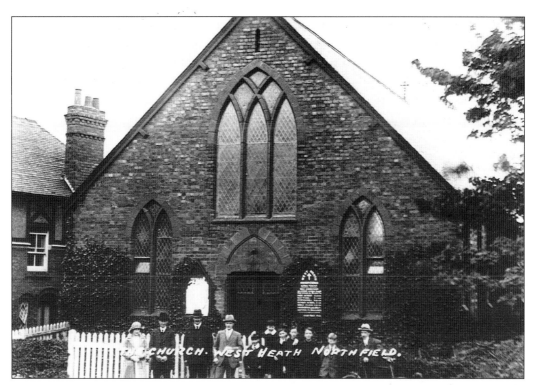

A smashing shot of worshippers standing outside the Church of Saint Anne, West Heath, sometime in the 1920s. Thanks to the Northfield Society. This place of worship resembled a village hall and was opened as a mission room belonging to Saint Nicolas, Kings Norton in 1900. Standing at the cross-roads of on the corner of Lilley Road and Alvechurch Road, it served both as a place of worship and as a meeting room for the parishioners. Located in the south west of the old manor of Kings Norton and in Worcestershire until 1911, West Heath was just what its name stated – a piece of heathland in the west. At the end of the 1700s, that heathland was enclosed to form West Heath Farm, Ivy House Farm and Hayes Farm. The area remained overwhelmingly rural until the twentieth century and as late as 1914, it boasted little more than an isolation hospital and a hamlet on and about Lilley Lane.

During the Second World War, one of the vicars of Saint Anne's was the Reverend W. Awdry, the man who brought us the Thomas the Tank Engine stories. After 1945, West Heath developed rapidly, close as it was to the expanding Longbridge factory, and now it is a populous suburb. Its church, that of Saint Anne's, gained the benefit of a new building in 1975 and is distinguished by its vast wooden vault.

Kathleen Hodgetts recalls that before the 'Man in the Moon' was built there was a big farm on the field opposite called The Hayes. It was owned by Mr and Mrs Workman who had four children. By their large house were two cottages: one for the herdsman and the other for the pig man who was Kathleen's father, Thomas Vale. He lived there 'with my mother, brother, sister and myself'. All of the children were born there. Billy went on the buses, Dulcie had a job at the Bath Tub and Kathleen went to work at Kings Norton School. Mr Vale showed Mr Workman's pigs and cows all over the big shows and 'nearly always gat first prizes for his big Whites and Black and White Pigs. Then they built the Man in the Mood and my Dad was one of the first in to get a free pint'. The Vales left West Heath to go with Mr Workman to another farm at Pershore, but Kathleen fondly recalls old friends like Mr and Mrs Hemings, Bobby Wright and Ken Ray

This is a cracking snap sent in by Enid Ellis of the Bath Tub, or the West Heath Lido as it was also known. During the Second World War, Enid was in the ARP Control Centre locally and spent many happy hours at the place. Built by Percy W. Hollier, the lido was part of a complex which included a fun fair, dance hall and chalets. It was the first such facility in Birmingham and had room for 10,000 people at an entrance fee of one shilling for adults and sixpence for children – for both swimming and dancing.

The Bath Tub was opened by Gracie Fields, who was appearing at the Hippodrome, at nine in the evening of July 1, 1937. It was estimated that more than 20,000 people came to this event at which Mantovani led his orchestra and over which Ronald Cartland presided. A cousin of the novelist Barbara Cartland, Ronald was part of the family of brassfounders which became the squires of Kings Heath from 1845, he himself was the MP for Kings Norton and Northfield and was to be killed fighting for his country in the Second World War.

Despite the great crowds at the opening and its attempts to be 'something different', the West Heath Lido was not a success and it was closed down just before the site was requisitioned for the war effort in late 1940. John Sermon actually won a talent contest at the Lido and was given a fountain pen 'as my prize and spent many happy days there with my family. When the war came, the Bath Tub was taken over as a munitions factory because in those days it was considered to be far out in the country. Mrs B. Moseley emphasises that the Bath Tub was the highlight of her childhood: 'my elder brother and I would save 2d a week for ages before we went. There was no fun to match sitting on the fountain in the middle of the Bath Tub with a big brother to look after you'.

several occasions, the fire watch of E. M. Lauze, H. Cox and E. J. Pickard bravely went into the inferno to bring out most of the valuable technical equipment.

Eddystone then moved to the Globe Works in Kent Street, which was the headquarters of its parent company Jarrett, Rainsford and Laughton and which had changed over to producing components for shells and mines as well as detonators, tubes, primers, pins and plugs. Unhappily, its main buildings were destroyed on November 19, 1940 and three day's later another of its works was blown up. So bad was the destruction that of the Eddystone equipment only two signal generators, one beat frequency oscillator and Q meter was saved. E. M. Lauze was again conspicuous by his courage and later was awarded the British Empire Medal.

Given the importance of Stratton it was vital that new and safer premises were found quickly. They were – at the Bath Tub, a lido in West Heath which also boasted a fun fair, dance hall and chalets. Stratton's was allocated the ladies' dressing rooms and the ballroom and the workers grafted almost ceaselessly to get production cracking. So successful were they that within three months output was greater than it had been before the Blitz.

Fortunately, Stratton's was not affected again by the enemy. During the war it made over four and a half million radio components for the British forces and over 4,500 transmitters, 7,264 receivers and 45,000 other additional pieces of equipment. Indeed, Eddystone two-way radio equipment provided a vital cross-channel link during the first British landings on D Day and the company also played an important part in the production of radar equipment – a weapon which was 'so successful in the prosecution of the war'.

Stratton's continued with its pioneering work after the Second World War and in 1965 it was sold to the Marconi Company, upon which its name became Eddystone Radio Limited. More recently, Eddystone has manufactured FM transmitters for the BBC and many other broadcasters and has been involved in developing the DAB system. The company remained at the Bath Tub site until 1996 when it relocated to new premises elsewhere in the city. It is a success story which emphasises the adaptability of Brummie manufacturers, the skills of their workers and the ongoing importance of manufacturing industry.

Lanes Lost in the Mist of Time: The Lost Streets of Brum

They're our road to the past – the forgotten lanes and alleys of Old Brum. A little-known feature in the Lozells area 'now lost forever since the building of Hotel School' is recalled by Mr A T Smith. It was Furnace Lane, a 'cobble-stoned alleyway about 10 feet wide which started near the corner of Gower Street and Guildford Street and ran south east for about half a mile, crossing Gerrard Street, then going up the hill crossing Clifford Street and finally ending at its junction with Porchester Street.'

Furnace Lane was inaccessible to motor vehicles and on the West Side ran behind houses in Guildford Street. On the East Side it gave access to the gardens and fronts of a row of cottages. After crossing Gerrard Street, the lane flanked houses built on the West Side, 'finally ending alongside some factory buildings at the Porchester Street end.' Mr Smith wonders whether the lane was named after a furnace. Well, it was. Aston Furnace stood at the corner of Porchester Street and Furnace Lane and was noted first in 1615 when Lozells and Aston was farmland and when Summer Lane ran through fields from its starting point at the bottom of Snow Hill.

Scotland Passage in 1935. Running between High Street and Moor Street, this was the narrowest through passage in Birmingham. Going down the passage was the deck for goods for the Birmingham Co-op, next to the 'Bodega' wine pub.

But the place was not a mill. It was where the water from Hockley Brook was used to work the furnace. For a number of years, it was associated with William Cowper or Cooper, hence Cowper Street, and was later used by the Jennens family in connection with Bromford Forge. The building was used until 1865 and gave its name to the strangely shaped and narrow Furnace Lane which survived into the twentieth century.

William Billard asks whether AB Row signified Aston Birmingham. Yes, it certainly did. The continuation of Coleshill Street to Belmont Row, AB Row is the shortest street name in Brum and once indicated part of the boundary between the parishes of Aston and Birmingham. For a long time, one of the houses in AB Row had a stone set in its front wall. On it was engraved the inscription 'A+B 1764.' It is likely that the stone stood on the ground until the area was developed in the late eighteenth and early nineteenth centuries.

On Pye's map of 1795, a house called BA is indicated opposite Duke Street but at this time AB Row was not named and instead Prospect Row ran all the way down to Coleshill Street. It seems that AB Row itself emerged in the mid-1800s: it is not shown on the 1839 Map of the Society for the Diffusion of Useful Knowledge, but is mentioned in White's Directory of 1850. The house in which the boundary stone was set was knocked down in the post-1945 redevelopment of Birmingham and the site was taken over by Gabriel and Company, whose factory had been at the rear of AB Row. This firm specialises in stainless steel products and put the stone in its front entrance. Recently, the business was relocated and the stone was handed back to the City of Birmingham.

Until 1838, Deritend was also in Aston, and near to the bridge over the River Rea between Digbeth and Deritend was a building called AB House – once again signifying the border between Birmingham and Aston. William also wonders about another building in the locality. In the 1940s and 1950s it stood on an island opposite Gabriel's and was surrounded by A B Row, Belmont Row and Coleshill Street. It was an old burned out market hall 'and as a lad I worked in the building'. It was used by the 'Boro Billposting Company' and William was a young poster fixer bill poster.

The building was originally opened as a market hall in 1837 by Messrs Robins following on from the development of the Duddeston Row neighbourhood. There is a story that the business first attempted to cover the old open air market at Gosta Green. Bits of a new building were put up, and as quickly they were taken down by the local people who resented the proposed new facility. Consequently, Messrs Robins fastened on a new site. This market did not succeed and the building was soon given over to other users.

K. Hiles states that on his way to work in the city centre he passes along High Street. On his way he sees Castle Street, 'which is about 20 yards long and leads to a double set of doors between Marks and Spencer and the MMEX warehouse.' As a thoroughfare it has no use to the public and I've been asked to explain for what purpose it is still maintained as a street. I don't think that there is a purpose for Castle Street remaining as a street. Simply, it is an old street which was all but swept away by the forming of the Inner Ring Road and the section which remains has never been closed off.

Castle Street used to run parallel with Carrs Lane, going from High Street to Moor Street, and it emerged from the coach-yard of the 'Castle' Inn. Originally, the pub was known as the 'Reindeer', but it changed its name in the early 1700s. Before that date, the street was known as Reindeer Foredrove, and had been a lane leading from High Street and through meadows towards Mole Street – the modern Moor Street. A number of other streets also took their names from pubs including Cannon Street and Jamaica Row (the bottom end of which once was Balsall Street) which recalls the 'Black Boy' – itself named after the swarthy-skinned Charles II.

Lover's Walk in Aston in 1954

Lover's Walk is another fascinating street name. A narrow route, it ran alongside the railway line from the Lichfield Road to Aston Hall Road and was apparent from the mid-1800s. It is likely that it recalls the courting couples who used to walk up and down what was a lane at the time when Aston was transforming itself from a rural outskirts of Birmingham into a major industrial town in its own right.

This photograph itself was taken in March 1954 and showed the marine stores of Martha Davies. It evokes powerful memories for John W. Turley. He was born in Lovers Walk in 1923 at number 4 Provident Cottages, a group of small houses which backed on to the woodyard. The house belonged to John's Gran (on his dad's side) and she had lived there for a number of years. Her husband had died in 1896 of typhoid, or, as Gran put it "Typhoo Fever". It put me off tea for a while. He was 39 and Gran was 36. She was left with eight children. My dad had been born in 1895 and so would have been just under one year old. There was no widow's pension or family allowance in 1896 and so Gran had to manage as best she could by cleaning and taking in washing. One of my aunts once told me that she remembered seeing her mother doing washing up at the old brewhouse with icicles hanging from her skirt.'

A local baker on the Lichfield Road used to let John's Gran have stale bread left over from the previous day's baking. John's aunts referred to the shop in the photograph of Lover's Walk as belonging to 'Old Tot' and 'I remember buying a book from out of the window. It was "Treasure Island" and it cost me two pence. There was also a sweet shop further along the road towards the main road.'

Mrs A Cox, nee Cope, also recalls Totty Ward, the local rag and bone lady. She kept her horse in the shed at the back of the premises and it would kick all night. There was also a bootmaker in the Walk called Mr Barr, a huge man with a big moustache, and nearby was the Ten Arches Mission and 'we all went there to Sunday School and brownies and scouts'. On the railway and just out of the picture 'lived a well known local lady known to us all as Polly on the railway. She was in charge of the pumping station.'

Mrs Cox used to take her mother for a walk up Lovers Walk each morning because 'my Mom had lost her eyesight and me being the last one of five kids to start school, it was my job at four years of age to do this'. The railway 'was a blessing to our Mom because she learned to tell the time by the trains and when the Pines Express went past a 3.20 p.m. she knew it was time to expect us home from school at 4 o'clock.' Nearby, on the corner by the bridges, was Mrs Goode's coffee house where you could get a cup of tea, sandwiches and 'jam or apple tarts which were always delicious'. Amongst the local folk were the Cashs, Teddy Priest, Edwin Wortly, Gladys Pettiver, Gladys and Leslie Timms and Billy and Joan Sedgley. And as Mrs Cox stresses, 'we all had so little yet so much'.

Harvey Barr's attention was drawn by the bay windows on the left of the photo – for in one of them lived his grandfather, William Joseph Barr, who was the local bootmaker. He moved into Lovers Walk in 1891 and set up his business when he was just 16. Four years later his mom died and William was left in charge of five brothers – three of whom were sent to the orphanage. In 1911, William moved to Park Road, Aston and set up as a corn market whilst his brother, Arthur, took over the boot repair shop. He stayed there until he died in 1959.

At his corn shop, Harvey's granddad had a horse and cart and during the First World War the horse was sent to war. Surprisingly it came back unscathed and 'it is said that all the neighbours lined the road to cheer the horse home. My grandfather vowed that the horse would never work again and it was put out to grass in Lea Marston where it died.'

For Albert Weaver the photograph brings to mind the days when he was five – and he's now in his 90s. He knew Lovers Walk as a short cut to Aston Lane and it was very busy 'when Pat Collin's Fair was on at what was called the Serpentine Grounds'. Albert's family were the caretakers at the Crown Works nearby and his pal, Harry Wait, lived in Lovers Walk itself. Another mate was Alfred Byron of the Lichfield Road, who lived at the back of Kate's coffees shop.

Little Bow Street in the 1920s – the only street in Birmingham with no through way. Mrs B Queen was born in Irving Street and her home was just across from Speaking Stile Walk – 'what a lovely name.' She remembers that there were back-to-back houses on the one side and factories on the other, Rogers and Wilson among them. Mrs Queen and her brothers and sisters went to St Thomas's School in Bath Row, just beyond which was Chequer's Walk. It is no longer there, nor is Little Bow Street 'which had steps leading down to Horsefair in Bristol Street.' Mr S. Fisher mentions that he used to work for Rogers and Wilson's, who made tyre moulds for motor vehicles and bicycles. The premises were located on the corner of Irving Street and a narrow, cobble-stoned passage know as Speaking Stile Walk – probably my favourite Brummagem street name.

Len Lloyd lived nearby in Chequer's Walk in a row of houses called Bath Cottages. They were situated behind Davenport's Brewery and the old Acci, which then was called the Queen's Hospital. I've got no idea as to why Chequer's Walk was so named, but I

can help with most of the other street names mentioned by Mrs Queen and Len. Irving Street and the nearby Washington Street were named after the American Author Washington Irving, who wrote Rip Van Winkle in Hockley. He did so while staying with his sister and brother-in-law, the Van Warts. Later they moved to Calthorpe Road, just off Five Ways and not far from Irving Street and were visited there by the famous writer.

Originally, it was a field path to Edgbaston and was known as Echo Hill Lane. This name arose from the fact that there was a stile at the top of the path by Holloway Head and from which 'an exceedingly clear echo could be raised.' Later on, Echo Hill Lane became Speaking Stile Walk because the stile 'spoke' when there was an echo.

Mrs D. Dyer writes of the smallest street in Brum – Silver Street. This ran from Dalton Street down to a passage at the back of Stafford Street Shops. You could park about three cars in it. You're right, Mrs Dyer, Silver Street was just 26 yards long and was the shortest street in Brum. Mrs Dyer also notes that the 'actual Bull Ring which they tied bulls to was up an entry at the side of W. H. Smith, which was just round the corner from Moor Street where I used to live. My father took me to see it before the war. I expect it was taken away when they cleared up after the bombs.'

Chapter 4:

Hard Collar

Rubber at the Fort: Dunlop

It was a right game to get to the new Dunlop factory in Erdington – for, a course, the Tyburn Road was yet to be cut. You was alright up to 'The Muckman's' pub at the foot of Gravelly Hill, but then you had to strike out eastwards along the cut till you come to the junction of Wheelwright Road and Bromford Lane – and then you could hop it along Wood Lane to the factory. With such a jaunt to and from work, no wonder that after a bit the company put on narrow boats for the workers to jump on at Salford Bridge, Aston and to take them all the way along the Birmingham and Fazeley Canal to Fort Dunlop.

Mind you, you had to agree that it was a most impressive place. Like Cadbury's chocolate works at Bournville, Fort Dunlop was a factory in a garden – well, more like a factory in the fields. Because if Wood Lane Farm disappeared as a result of its building, then The Fort was flanked still to the east by Ashold Farm and to the south by the River Tame and the Birmingham Racecourse. And then to the west, was the great sewage farm of the Birmingham, Tame and Rea District Drainage Board.

The new factory highlighted the rapid rise of the Dunlop Rubber Company. It had emerged out of a small concern, the Pneumatic Tyre Company, which had been formed to develop John Boyd Dunlop's patent for a pneumatic tyre – a product which transformed the manufacture of wheels and allowed cyclists to ride more smoothly and with less vibration.

Beginning in Belfast, the business soon moved to Dublin, but after complaints about the smell of rubber – essential for the production of pneumatic tyres – it shifted to Coventry. Led by members of the dynamic du Cros family from Ireland, swiftly the business came to control almost all rights to make pneumatic tyres. At this stage, these goods were hand made from rubber which was bought in and it was realised that if the company were to expand successfully then it needed to own its own rubber supply.

This was provided by the purchase in 1896 of the India rubber tyre part of a rubber company owned by three Irish Brummies, the Byrne Brothers, on the Lichfield Road in Aston. The premises were called the Para Mills and tyre making was moved here from Coventry. Production relied upon a Doughty Press which reduced the time needed for tyre moulding and vulcanising from two hours to three minutes. As Arthur du Cros declared, now 'tyres could be turned out like shelling peas'.

Four years later, the newly-formed Dunlop Rubber Company Limited took over the

This is a marvellous shot of workers arriving by narrow boat at the new Fort Dunlop in Erdington in 1918.

    Christine Bartlett's mother actually worked for The Dunlop when the firm was at Aston Cross and 'she told me that when the wind was in the right direction the workers received the combined smell of rubber, beer and HP Sauce. As a comptometer operator in the Wages Department she moved to Fort Dunlop when it relocated to Erdington. In those days, the act of counting out the workers' wages in cash each week left them with totally blackened fingers. Shortly before the Great War, my father came from Hereford to work as an accountant in the same department. They married in 1918 when he was serving as a soldier. After the war they lived in one of the wooden houses provided by the firm, on what was the Castle Bromwich Aerodrome, now Castle Vale. There was a bus service to Erdington three times a week; my Dad got to work on a motorbike. When the Tyburn Road housing estate was built the family lived there.' As Christine stresses, The Dunlop was a family firm and both she and her brother were also employed there in the Technical Photographic Section.

rest of the rubber-making aspects of the Byrne Brothers at their Manor Mills in Salford Street, Nechells. Keen to be involved in anything to do with vehicle manufacture, the du Cros family also played a major role in the founding of Longbridge by Herbert Austin.

    The rise of Dunlop was spectacular and by 1909 it had its own rubber plantations in Malaya, a factory in Japan where it made rickshaw and bicycle tyres and it was also producing golf balls and aviation tyres. Unsurprisingly, conditions became cramped in its mills and in May 1915 was turned 'the first sod of that stronghold of the tyre industry' – Fort Dunlop. This new venture encompassed 260 acres bought from Birmingham Corporation and soon it gained a world-wide reputation not only for the superb quality of its goods but also for its innovative research into rubber-based and synthetic rubber products.

Mrs B. R. Caine's late husband finished his National Service in the early 1950s and from that time was employed at Fort Dunlop until he was forced to retire in 1984 due to health problems. This particular photo shows youngsters of workers enjoying a children's Christmas Party at The Fort in the early 1960s. Two of Mrs Caine's older children are on the photo.

Frank Southall worked at Fort Dunlop for 21 years from 1926 and has related something which was not known generally: that The Dunlop sponsored the formation of a Territorial Army Unit, the 225 Field Company Royal Engineers. This comprised of about 60 men who all worked at The Dunlop and was formed in 1934/5. Annual camps were held in rotation at Bournemouth, Christchurch, Weymouth and Bournemouth again. When war was declared all of the lads were called up and many of them were together at Dunkirk.

Now 83, Betty Humphries went to Fort Dunlop aged 16, straight from King Edward's Grammar School, Camp Hill. She worked at invoicing on the Racing Section and was paid £1 a week. Racing drivers would ring up with a specification for new tyres and 'we used to enjoy the urgency to put through the invoices'. Betty recalls strongly the overpowering smell of rubber 'which was pretty awful' and that the company had a 'splendid running track' upon which one of her friends, Winifred Jefferies, won many medals.

Dr David H. Twiss grandfather, Dr Douglas Twiss DSc, was the first and only research chemist employed by the Dunlop Rubber Company. He joined in 1912 and worked for the firm until 1946, 'by which time he had developed a fully equipped research unit and had very many people working under him. Over 200 patents were attributed to him, over half of which related to latex'.

By the late 1950s, Dunlop owned 94 factories across the world and employed 100,000 people. But Fort Dunlop lay at its heart. Dominated by the huge landmark of the base stores, it boasted not only superb research and manufacturing capabilities but also sports fields and training schools for apprentices. Importantly, it gave work to over 10,000 men and women, over a quarter of whom had 25 years or more service. This exemplified one of the successes of The Fort: for all its great size, it was a family concern with generation after generation of family members following each other into employment.

Tragically, over the last few years and for various reasons, production at Fort Dunlop has declined greatly and recently many workers have been laid off. Neither their hardships nor their skills and capabilities should be forgotten. They are tyre makers par excellence and can still produce the products desired by the world if given the opportunity. This article is dedicated to them – the men and women of Fort Dunlop. They are the people who transformed a small company into one of the greatest manufacturing concerns in the world.

In 1984, Japanese managers from Sumitomo Rubber Industries, the new owners of Dunlop, visited The Fort. On their tour of the plant they were guided by Ken Roberts (third from left) and here they are watching Mr Alderman Brown construct a truck tyre. The Japanese men are, from the left, Mr K. Nishimara and Mr Fumiki Okamoto. Thanks to the **Birmingham Evening Mail.**

The Darbys are a family deeply connected with the history of Fort Dunlop, for a number of them worked at the factory: Young Jim, Fred Junior, Leonard, Fred Darby Senior and his brother

Jim. It was Fred who began the connection of the Darbys with Dunlop. His grandson, Kevin, still has a reference from the Dunlop Rubber Company, then based at Aston Cross, which was dated July 4, 1914 and which states that Fred 'has been in our employment for two years, during which time we found him honest, industrious and sober'. The reference was signed by the famous Arthur Du Cros, a leading member of the family that was responsible for the spectacular growth of the Dunlop business.

Born at 17, Freeman Street in 1892, Frederick Darby joined the 9th Battalion the Royal Warwickshire Regiment in April 1915 and served at Gallipoli, Mesopotamia and Baku. After his discharge in 1919, he and his brother, Sidney James, both found jobs at The Fort. A few years later, Fred and his wife, Elizabeth, went to live at Gravelly Hill, close to his work. At The Dunlop, Fred was for many years a foreman in the packing section and rose to take charge of that area. Indeed, it was stated in the Dunlop News Letter *that what Fred 'does not know about preparing Dunlop tyres and other goods for export, or for despatch to destinations in Britain, would not amount to very much'.*

Fred's brother, Jim, also spent most of his working life at Fort Dunlop – at the company's Depot, which was part of the Base Stores. In charge of The Depot, and under the packing room control of his father was Young Jim, son of Fred. The family involvement was made up by Fred Junior, a skilled operative packer, and Leonard, who worked on the Base Stores loading bay. Dunlop rose to greatness because of the skills and hard work of families such as the Darbys. Their contribution to the well being of Birmingham should not be overlooked.

Patrick Ryan started at the firm in 1959 and although he was there for only twelve months, The Fort made a big impression upon him. He was just sixteen years old when he came to Brum from Pallasgreen in County Limerick, Ireland and his job at Dunlop was his first in England. When he applied for work at the great tyre factory, Patrick stated that was eighteen so that he would get the full wages of £10 per week. He was put in a section that was called The Mill but which was known by the workers as the Black Hole. This was the shop where all the raw materials were milled into rubber. It was hard work 'and we got a choice of two cold drinks – milk or orange – every shift and we also had a paid half hour at the end of each shift for a shower'. Patrick got on very well at The Fort and enjoyed working there, but because the personnel department insisted on seeing his birth certificate he had to leave.

By contrast, Kathleen Millichamp's mother worked at The Fort for over twenty years. Her name was Julia Thompson and she was one of the women who was employed at the old Manor Mills in Aston and was transferred to the new factory in Erdington. In fact, Julia was the first woman to make the first solid tyre and 'she had her name in the office in gold letters'. When she was on nights, Julia used to go to work on the canal boat. The family lived in Argyle Street, Aston and after Julia had put her children to bed she set off and 'we used to wave to her from the bedroom window'. In those days, the area around The Fort was all fields but when Julia came home 'she used to smell awful from the naphtha with which they made the tyres'.

Precious Talents of Jewellery Men and Women: The Jewellery Quarter

It had come as a shock to him. He'd only been to big newish factories, packed with workers and powered by electricity. No wonder that this place amazed him. It couldn't have been a bigger contrast with the modern facilities he was used to. In fact at one point he'd almost rubbed his eyes, as if he was dreaming and had stepped into a scene from a Charles Dickens novel.

The first thing which had thrown him was the look of the premises. It didn't seem like somewhere to work. Instead, it appeared to be a house and so did all the other buildings in the street. They were a bit down-at-heel but they were still substantial structures and some of the doorways were quite ornate. It was apparent that they'd been built for the wealthy of Brum, yet there was no indication that rich people lived in them now.

Even though he realised this, and even though he noticed that the footpaths were full of workfolk scurrying hither and thither, he still felt a bit foolish as he approached the entrance. But he knew he'd got it right when he saw a brass name plate telling of the businesses which were to be found inside. There was a gold chain manufacturer, an engraver, a guilder, a diamond mounter, a setter, and a gem ring maker. He found it hard to believe that all these people were based in what was basically a six roomed house, yet it was obvious that they were.

Walking into a narrow passage, he noticed that there were men collaring in the rooms on either side. Glancing at the piece of paper in his hand to check his directions, he realised that he had to go to the first floor. As he went up the rickety and creaky stairs he minded out for the gaps which could lead you to trip and come a purler. When he reached the landing there were another two rooms, and he saw that the firm he was after was on the right. He pushed the door and to his surprise it opened. That struck him as really peculiar. There he was in a decaying building filled with men working with precious stones and metals and yet no one seemed to lock their doors. Wasn't it dangerous not to have entrances barricaded and windows shuttered? He found out later that there was no fear of robberies nor worries about violence.

When he walked in the room everyone carried on with their tasks. There were three men sitting at an unusually shaped workbench. It was quite wide and each of the blokes was hunched over a semi-circle cut into the wood, beneath which hung a leather pouch. He was fascinated by what he saw. The bench was cluttered with tins, trays and bottles full of liquid – whether it was water or acid he couldn't tell. A small piece of wood jutted out from the bench and beneath it hung a rack on which could be seen a variety of tools.

His eyes darted all over the place but they were drawn to a strange sight. One of the men appeared to be breathing flames! His curiosity forced him to a closer look and he realised that between his lips the craftsman had a thinnish metal rod down which he blew. Using his mouth in this way, he directed gas flames onto a ring, which he held with a tool. With his free hand he manipulated another metal instrument to fashion the ring. At last, one of the men looked up. The young man told him his business and then went on his way, determined to write an article on the ancient skills and ways of Birmingham's Jewellery Quarter.

Joyce Allen's family were thoroughly immersed in the Jewellery Quarter. Her maiden name is Ford and here Rosie Ford is polishing at the firm of P. H. Bunting, manufacturing jeweller's of Hylton Street.

Mick Bickerton, a stalwart of Bickerton Jewellery, still in Vyse Street brings to mind how when he started work in the Jewellery Quarter in 1950 the workshop hadn't changed from its 1864 origins. He wishes that he'd 'listened to the memories of the First World War of the old craftsmen but I'd switch off when they started reminiscing at W. H. Small in Pitsford Street where I was an apprentice. I was by far the youngest on the premises and recall the wooden floor boards, full of cracks, where bits of gold and jewellery would fall through at times and remain undisturbed for years. Most times we never looked for the smaller remnants. These men were on piecework and it wasn't worth their while. If it were a bigger piece, the men would have to pay for it! They sat at circular benches and were rarely allowed into the office. Indeed, they weren't even allowed through the front door.' In the early '20's, I heard, there was a boss who'd ride his horse against the tide of workers running up Vyse Street to go home at 6pm. He'd use his whip against them if they got in his way. One poor soul worked as a porter after being shell-shocked in World War Two. He'd shake and raise his arm as if he would strike us – but we were told he imagined he was back in the army and was trying to salute.'

And what capabilities and expertise there were! Orders came to Brum from across the world, pulled in by the artistry and dexterity of the city's jewellery workers. These were the people who took gold and silver and shaped it into things of beauty. These were the people who grasped precious stones and formed them into objects of desire. Sharp of eye and deft of hand, generations of them had grafted in their small workshops, passing on their lore to sons and daughters and ensuring that their traditions would go on.

These exceptional folk were all adept at one aspect of their trade. That's why they gathered close to each other so that goods could be passed easily from one specialist to another. From at least the middle of the 1800s they had congregated in that part of Hockley bounded by Great Charles Street, Icknield Street, the Sandpits, Key Hill and Livery Street. Their successors are still there – making sure that the Jewellery Quarter keeps its reputation for talent and creativity. Birmingham's hidden gem.

This is another photograph from the collection of Joyce Allen nee Ford. It is a wonderful shot of activity in a jewellery workshop. Ken Ford is standing.

Avis Wilson has memories memory of her late father, Frederick Massingham, who started his own business in Augustus Street, later moving in with his brother James in Northampton Street: 'they had an upstairs "shop", so dilapidated that the stairs were unsafe. The two rooms, one an "office" and one a workshop, had more papers stuffed in the windows than glass. There was an open stove. I thought it marvellous'.

All of the family of Mrs Margaret Farrand worked in the Jewellery Quarter until her parents married in about the 1920s: 'when father came back from World War One, his job as a musical instrument-maker had gone, so off he went to Vyse Street and thereabouts for work. My mother was book-keeper for Jabez Wolfe of Vyse Street and she'd tell me how all the floor sweepings were sifted for gold-dust each evening. Come 7pm each evening, a messenger would take the post in a basket-carriage to the Post Office. Thousands of pounds and no security firms then!'

A craftsman at work in the Jewellery Quarter.

W. H. Huckfield once had a part-time job at Turner and Simpson's in Legge Lane, where 'my brother and I worked in the office helping to wrap up medals ready for taking down to the post office. We used to race along Albion Street down Frederick Street, then jump on our basket trolley and ride all the way down New Hall Hill just in time to catch the post office before it closed. This firm almost became a family affair as my two sisters and a brother and their partners all worked there.'

Marjorie Ell, nee Shenton, lived in the Jewellery Quarter from 1918 until the outbreak of the Second World War 'when I came into the country as a land girl'. Her mother kept a shop on the corner of Hockley Street and Vyse Street. It was 'a proper general stores. She used to make jugs of tea for the work people, ham and cheese sandwiches, cakes, bread pudding and dinners. I went to St. Paul's School and in my dinner time had to take the dinners to various workshops.' When Marjorie left school she went to work at G. H. Johnstone's in Northampton Street. They made cufflinks and 'I was taught to enamel them in stripes for the public schools and regiments. A man in the shop would paint the crest on the other side. and when they were linked together made a beautiful article. We had a gypsy party every year and a charabanc would come and take us in the country. When anyone was 21, the workers from the other shops in the factory would some to drum you out. They would bring dustbin lids, old saucepans and anything that would make a noise and beat it for 5 mins. Every so often we had new floor boards so that they could burn the old ones to get the gold dust from them.'

A Grocer of Distinction: George Mason

George Mason was an extraordinary man whose enthusiasm, drive and business ability led to the emergence of one of the biggest grocery firms in the Midlands and North of England. The son of a Shropshire farmer, he came into the grocery trade early on, having been apprenticed to Brittain's of Newport – a noted grocer's in the county. George Mason soon made an impact, becoming first a manager at the Oakengates branch and then manager of the whole company.

Following this rapid rise and in the late nineteenth century, he was appointed as manager of Probert Williams and Co. of West Bromwich. Here he teamed up with Frank C. Hammond, the company secretary. Formerly with a firm of solicitors in the Black Country, in 1893 Frank Hammond had become cashier and confidential clerk to the grocery and paper business of William Watkin Heelis at 183-185, High Street, West Bromwich – which was taken over four years later by Probert Williams and Co.

After the retirement of Mr Probert, George Mason became a director and the name of the company was changed to Mason Williams and Co. Under Mason's leadership, the business expanded rapidly in the Black Country but it was obvious that the Shropshire man had a hunger for starting up a new concern – as did Frank Hammond. Thus in 1909 the two men left their positions and accepted an offer to join forces with a large, London-based provision importer – J. and J. Lonsdale Ltd.

Obviously, the owners of the metropolitan firm were impressed by the combination of Mason and Hammond. The Shropshire man was someone with an intimate knowledge of the grocery trade and had shown his ability to improve and expand a company swiftly; whilst the Black Country chap was someone who had made plain his clever administrative skills and business acumen.

Lonsdale's proprietors were proved correct in their shrewd assessment. Backed by the London concern's cash, within a few weeks Mason and Hammond had opened up their first shops in Wednesbury and Walsall. A fortnight later, they began trading in West Bromwich and by the end of the year they had 24 shops under the name of George Mason's.

From the start, Mason and Hammond adopted two policies: first to buy other, well-established companies; and second to sell all groceries, but especially butter and cheese, at keen prices. The enthusiastic public response to their pricing strategy justified their approach, so much so that the expansion of the new company was remarkable. By 1914 it had taken over the longer-established Mason Williams and Co. and boasted more than 100 shops – and a year later it made its presence felt in South Wales when it joined forces with a respected local grocery chain.

Because of the rapid growth of Mason's, the head office and warehouses in Thynne Street, West Bromwich became inadequate and so in 1922 the company relocated its headquarters to a block of buildings in Bradford Street. The growth of Mason's continued unhindered and it opened up new branches not only in Birmingham and the West Midlands but also it acquired grocery businesses in Manchester and the north west of England. George Mason himself died in 1934, by which date the company which bore his name had 388 stores.

After Mason's death, the Lonsdale family sold their control in the company to The International Tea Company's Stores Ltd, which also took over the whole of the financial interests of George Mason. Goods from the factories and bakeries of International soon flowed into the Mason's shops but the company did continue to trade as an independent entity under the chairmanship of Frank Hammond, who was also the managing director.

At the outbreak of the Second World War, George Mason's employed over 4,000 people and had a fleet of 150 vehicles which 'maintains its transport facilities, keeping

This snap was taken in 1948 outside the Kingstanding branch of George Mason's on Brandywood Road. It shows George Place, who is on the left. Next to him is Renee Brown, then Doreen Argyle and a young lady whose name George cannot recall. The manageress was Miss Satchwell and was inside the shop. George started work as an apprentice in the branch aged fourteen in 1947. He still has his indentures which show that he was to receive 22 shillings a week for the first six months of his time, 27s 6d during the second six months, 32 shillings during the second year and 37s 6d at the end of his three year apprenticeship.

Albert Young worked at George Mason's from February 1, 1954 until the demise of the firm in the mid-1970s. He began as a stocktaker and later became a retail executive. When stocktaking 'we would travel to stores Monday to Wednesday by bus or train depending on the location. Thursdays and Fridays were spent collating our three days work and then taking stock in the warehouse for the company's buyers. The main Mason's offices and warehouse was on the corner of Bradford Street and Birchall Street and across the yard was the building where the cooked meats were produced and from which also operated Kearley and Tongue, a wholesale supplier.' The reception area to the offices themselves was controlled by ex-sergeant major Mr Ford from the Corps of Commissionaires.

A cracking shot of the George Mason's branch at 169, High Street, Harborne in September 1956.

Anthony Jinks recalls that as a child he took a grocery order to the George Mason's shop on the Stratford Road, Shirley and one thing has always stayed in his mind since: this was 'the way in which cash was transported to the cashier's office from the counter. Cash was put in a wooden pot, which was screwed on to a guide suspended from the ceiling. A cord was then pulled and the guide was then sent down a catenary wire direct to the cashier's office.' The journey was then reversed when any change was sent back. Anthony has also sent me a copy of a grocery list made out by his mom on a Mason's order sheet. Dated September 9, 1959 it indicates that 2lb sugar was 1s $3\frac{1}{2}$ d; 2lbs of self raising flour was 1s 4d; a tin of peaches was 1s 7d; and a packet of assorted biscuits was 1s $4\frac{1}{2}$ d.

Joan Stott was just fourteen when she started work at the Mason's store in High Street, Birmingham and she was actually in the cash desk with her cousin – receiving the money sent on the wire. They were long hours for a young person, and Joan did not finish until 7 o'clock on a Thursday night , 8 o'clock on a Friday evening and 9 o'clock on a Saturday night. From High Street, Joan went to work at the shop in Harborne and then was moved on to the office in Bradford Street. During the Second World War she remembers that one day 'I walked down the Bull Ring amidst the rubble and arrived at George Mason's to find it badly damaged. The store rooms at the back had been hit. We sorted out what we could in the office and eventually moved to school premises in Kings Heath – but I shall never forget the chaos of that morning.'   Aged twelve in the mid-1930s, Len Taylor gained what he had longed for when a became a delivery boy for Mason's on The Lane, the Ladypool Road. It was a bicycle! Although it was a bit heavy because of the carrier on the front, it meant that no more did Len have to hire a bike for a penny an hour from Burns' on the Stoney Lane. On top of that he was paid seven bob a week, an enormous increase over the three and a tanner he'd earned as a newspaper boy. The work was enjoyable although the hours were long. Produce such as sugar and various dried fruits were weighed and bagged within the store. This proved to be Len's difficulty for he was despatched to fetch a bundle of green, brown and red wrappers from the stock room, 'a daunting task for someone colour blind. Never to be admitted to anyone. After several aborted attempts I think the manageress realised I had a problem and fetched them herself. My thanks to any of the staff who may still be around.'

all shops adequately supplied with fresh commodities from the refrigerating and air-conditioned rooms of the immense central warehouse, and carrying out that personal service to customers which is such an important phase of modern business methods – household delivery'.

During the winter of 1940-41 , the Bradford Street headquarters was hit three times by bombs. Operations were moved to Institute Road, Kings Heath until 1945 when the main offices and warehouses were functional again.

George Mason's continued to trade strongly in the post-war years, but in 1972-73 its accounts were integrated with those of International. Then in 1975, the name George Mason disappeared as its stores became part either of Pricerite or International. At the same time a new International depot was opened in Halesowen. Still, George Mason's may be gone, but many remember fondly its high levels of service and quality food.

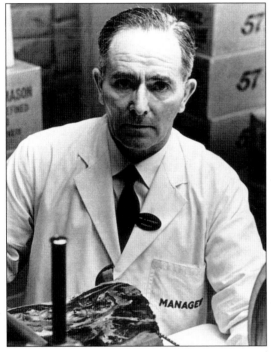

Harold Sherriff was a Mason's stalwart. He started with the company in 1918, when he was an eleven-year old part-time errand boy and two years later began work full time at the Bordesley Green store. At the age of 22, Harold was promoted to manager – a post he held for 43 years. During his service, Harold was also chairman of the Midlands Division of the Shop Assistants Union for eleven years, he was on the Wages Council for six years and he was on the advisory committee for the College of Food and Domestic Art. This photograph shows Harold at work.

Dinah Painter, nee Batchelor, worked at George Mason's on the Bristol Road, Selly Oak between 1942 and 1944 and a time of food rationing. She patted butter and cut cheese to the exact weight per customer. There was a big demand for cracked eggs and damaged tins and everything was weighed into bags. The aptly-named Walter C. Mason travelled quite a few miles on his trusty errand boy's bike for the Mason's branch in Erdington High Street. He has vivid memories of many things, such as the occasion when he was about to deliver a busy Saturday grocery: 'gaily cocked on me bike, but I couldn't turn the handlebar because the cardboard box protruded above the bars. Alas a I made a ten foot scratch along a brand new tram just out of the depot.'

Lionel Miles Hull was also a delivery boy, in his case working each Friday night and Saturday for the Mason's branch on Cape Hill. One Friday there had been heavy snow and he was delivering groceries to Quinton. The snow was very thick on the road and Lionel had to push the fully-laden bike all the way. At about 8.15 'the assistant manager called on my mother to say that the manager was very angry as he was waiting to shut the shop. My mother, who was never backward in coming forward, in no uncertain terms that he could wait at our house for the bicycle as and when her son did come home because I would not be returning to the shop and they should have had more sense than to send me to Quinton in such weather – Good old Mom!'

Ale the Conquering Hero: Mitchell's and Butler's

He'd had enough and that was that. Things weren't working out in his apprenticeship and he wanted to pack it in, but he knew if he went back home to Hinckley then his father would be sure to give him a right dressing down. Times were hard in the Hungry 1840s and the last thing you did was to chuck away the chance of getting a trade. William Butler knew that and he realised that he was lucky to have a job of any kind when so many blokes were out of collar, not only here in Leicester but also in the country as a whole.

Still, he'd made his mind up and even though he may have been just 16 he was a youngster who put his mind, body and soul to it once he'd decided on a course of action. So with a firm resolve off he set. He only had a ha'penny in his pocket but he'd made sure he'd had a good feed before he ran away – for that's what he was, a runaway

Workers at Mitchell's and Butler's in 1913. Thanks to Les Richards.

    The maternal grandfather of R. D. Jones was Alfred Jefferies. In the 1920s he lived at the bottom of Heath Street, Winson Green, close to the old GKN bridge near to the border of Smethwick and Birmingham. He was a self-employed canal bargee and was contracted to convey 'spent' hops from Mitchell's and Butler's Brewery to farmers in the Lichfield area, where they were used on the land as fertiliser. Alfred's wife, Alice Maud, worked in the Accounts Department at M&B at the same time.

    Lilian Smith remembers when Mitchell's and Butler's had their own fire brigade. If there was a fire then the company would sound a hooter 'that was known as Mitchell's and Butler's Bull, you could hear it for miles. It was a sight to see, those beautiful shires come charging out, and those wonderful firemen in their shining brass helmets, and a fireman clanging a bell.' Lilian also recalls that if there was a carnival or fete on that M&B always sent a team of beautiful shires and drays. And you could always tell when the firm was brewing as 'you could smell the hops for miles and be sure of a good night's sleep'. When they lived in Shenstone Road, Lilian and her husband were told by an aged couple that in years gone by a brook had run nearby, across which deer had leaped to get on to Mitchell's and Butler's land. This was the reason why the business had their trade mark of a deer's leap.

Thelma Coulson has sent in this photo of her former father-in-law, Lennard Hayne. It shows him 'getting ready for a good dowsing of beer from all those who look as though they are going to drink his health but in reality will be pouring their drinks over him as he comes out of his apprenticeship. at the age of 21. This was approximately in 1931.' The third man on the right, away from Lennard, is his father who has come to watch and join in the fun., whilst 'it is thought that the man on the far right of the picture with the bowler hat on is either Mr Mitchell or Mr Butler… Len Hayne rose up through his years at the Brewery to become a Head Cooper and then foreman of the Cooperage before his retirement.' He played for M. and B.'s crown green bowling team 'and was a very well known player on the bowling circuit – as indeed is his son Peter Hayne'. Sadly, Lennard died in 1992 in his eighty-first year.

Mrs H. Turner used to live at the back of Mitchell's and Butler's and 'I well remember the workers going to work early mornings with their hooter blowing. They were allowed I think 4 minutes after this grace then the big wooden gates would shut. When I was a child before the war my father and neighbours would order a small barrel of beer, a firkin I think, for Xmas and all special occasions. My sister's 21st was in 1938 and as we lived up a big yard what a party we had with M & B's beer.' After the war, 'the lovely lights on M & B's wall which had been off for so long suddenly blazoned with light'.

apprentice. He knew where he wanted to go, it was to the dynamic town of Birmingham, but even this purposeful young man hadn't reckoned on what a traipse it was to get there. When he did arrive he was wore out, but he knew he had to get a job quickly. The hunger pains were beginning to scold his belly and if he got too weak he'd never be able to help himself.

Fortunately, he landed a place at a hairdresser's and soon after he took on a part-time job at the 'Crown' Inn along Broad Street. It was a big and busy boozer on one of the main drags into Brum and the hectic life of a publican seemed to appeal to William.

Mind you, he wasn't a youngster when he reckoned he ought to shift his life and take over a pub. Thirty-nine years old and married, he became the publican of the 'London Works' Tavern in Smethwick in 1866. There were plenty of factories about and William soon drew in a good crowd with his own home brew. In fact, he gained such a good reputation for the quality of his ales that in 1877 he was approached to go into partnership with the owner of the 'Crown' – the pub where once he'd been a barman.

William had as good a mind for business as he had an eye and taste for beer. He recognised the home brewing operations at the 'Crown' and then moved on to building a new brewery so that he could sell his beer to other publicans. It was a big place, with the capacity of 5,000 barrels a week and storage in the cellars for 10,000 barrels. But

Isabel and Charles Hill have sent me this bostin shot of Charles's brother, Rodian, going through his apprenticeship. Here he is kissing his mom, Mari Hill, whilst Isabel and Charles look on from the right.

Betty Gregory's first memory of M & B is of her mom telling her that her grandad worked there and she had to take a billycan of tea down to him with a hard boiled egg in the tea. He would inspect the egg and if there was any marks on it he would send it back. Betty herself brings to mind the 'strong smell of the hops and the bull sounding in the morning and dinner time. Also there was the memorial to the workers who had lost their lives in the 1st World War. It always seemed to have poppies on it. Then there were the lovely dray horses with their sparkling brasses which delivered the barrels of beer. The draymen would call at Bantis cafe in Grove Lane for a cup of tea and a bacon or sausage sandwich.'

Betty is the wife of the great amateur boxer Sam Gregory and remembers the Mitchell's and Butler's sign lit up in red – 'this, of course, was put out during the war, but after the war when the sign was lit up again it was very exciting. I remember I had first got engaged to Sam and walking past the M&B's sign I flashed my right to see diamonds'.

in fact, William Butler's operations were soon getting a bit too big for even that site and that's when he started to look around for a move so that he could extend his business. The opportunity for such an advance rose from joining forces with Henry Mitchell.

Back in 1851, Henry's dad, also called Henry, had taken over the 'Oddfellows Arms' in Hall Street, West Bromwich. It was a beerhouse, that is it could not sell wines and spirits, but within a year he had a full licence at the bigger 'Cape Inn', in Spon Lane. The place was right on the cut and Henry Mitchell offered well aired beds, good stabling and excellent wharfage at his premises. It's obvious that old man Mitchell was on the way up in the game, for in 1854 he took over the even larger 'Crown' on the Oldbury Road in Smethwick. It had two kitchens, a tap room, a bar, a malt room, two attics, a club room, a long water trough and four cellars. Soon after, Henry senior was joined by his son and from 1861 Henry junior was in charge of the business.

The younger man was keen on acting not only as a publican but also as a common brewer, selling his beers to other publicans, and he developed a popular Light Mild Ale. So much in demand was this and other brews that Henry was hard put to keep up with his orders. That's why he bought part of Fawdy's Farm on Cape Hill in 1878. He needed a bigger brewery and he was going to build it himself. Eight years later, the new brewery occupied 14 acres, it had an annual output of over three and a quarter million gallons and it gave work to 271 people. Despite his success, Henry Mitchell was keen to join forces with William Butler. Both men respected each other, both knew about beer and both knew they could do even better in partnership.

They did do even better after they came together in the late 1890s and today Bass's Cape Hill Brewery is a tribute to them and their workers.

Station to Station: Railway Workers

It was like a job on the corporation was a job on the railway. The pay may not have been high but it was regular work and so long as you did your bit properly and kept your nose clean, then you were there for life. And in an era when so much work was irregular, casual and part-time, it meant a lot to know just exactly how much was coming in to the house each week. That kind of knowledge allowed you to plan ahead and to have a concept of the future – a concept which was denied to so many workers who had to focus on what they could earn today and tomorrow let alone next week or next year.

Mind you, it wasn't a cushy number being a railwayman. You had to do your job conscientiously, keenly and well – because if you didn't there was always someone else ready to jump in and take your place. And there was plenty of hard collar involved. Just think of how those firemen had to strain might and main to shift shovel load after shovel load of coal into the fire so as to feed the ravenous appetite of the locomotive engine for steam. It might have captured your imagination to see the train speeding along the track, billowing vapour along the way, but its swiftness and charm was the result of graft and diligence.

The firemen belonged to one of the many groups encompassed within the term of railwaymen. At the pinnacle of their hierarchy of labour were the drivers. With overtime, some of them earned wages which matched or bettered those of small gaffers with their own factories and which certainly were higher than those of little shopkeepers.

Resplendent in their uniforms and with their buttons and shoes highly polished, drivers used to carry oval boxes made of leather. Inside, each box was separated into three sections: in the middle were cleaning cloths; on the one side were two glass tubes, which were spares for the steam pressure recorders in the cab of the locomotive; and on the other side was a tea bottle.

Like the drivers, the guards also had to be turned out immaculately. They were marked out by their sparkling and eye-catching watches which were hung on a chain and were carried in a waistcoat pocket. These watches were given to them by their companies and in the nineteenth century, they had been responsible both for the standardisation of time in Britain and for our modern idea of time.

Imagine it. Before the coming of the railways, a clock in Brum could show 10.00 a.m., whilst one in Smethwick would indicate five past ten, another in West Bromwich would give five to ten and yet one more in Oldbury would state that it was ten to ten. The lack of a recognised time across the nation was a major problem for railway companies. Their trains had to run to time, but that time had to be the same everywhere. So they put in clocks at their stations, gave their guards watches and set them according to Greenwich Mean Time.

A successful railway service was also dependent upon thousands upon thousands of men such as platelayers, labourers, cleaners, porters, clerks, inspectors and many

Albert Rippin has sent in this photo of his father which was taken at the Lawley Street stables of the LMS railway sometime during the inter-war years. Although his name was William, Mr Rippin was known by his mates as Jack. He worked in the stables from when he left school in 1916 until the late 1950s when he became a foreman at the Birmingham Print Market for British Rail until he retired because of ill health in 1966. In this shot you can see he is wearing gaiters (a covering of cloth or leather below his knees) to protect his legs from the rats which abounded in the stables and which often would jump up at the workers. In the background on the right is a horse trough and on the left is a horse cart.

For Albert, one of the highlights of the years was the May Day Parade at Calthorpe Park when the horses and carts were decorated and on one proud occasion he joined his dad on his turnout. On a Sunday, Albert would meet his dad in a coffee house by the stables where they would be joined by Holy Joe, the renowned preacher and tireless worker for the poor who lived in Lawley Street and was a famous character in the old Bull Ring. The two men would have billycans, condensed milk and some tea screwed up in paper ready to make a brew later in the day.

Alan Osborne's grandfather also was based at Lawley Street, in his case as a horse lorry man. He was John William Gilkes and he had come to Brum from the village of Haunton, just inside Oxfordshire: 'being a farm boy, he naturally went for a job with horses. He wasn't very tall, but was big across the shoulders with a 48′ chest. He could pick up three-quarters of a hundredweight (38kg) in his teeth, even into his 60s. He was involved in some of the early strikes, but told me that at one time he had to pay $\frac{1}{2}$d or 1d per load protection to the 'peaky blinders', depending upon the value of the load.'

Mr Gilkes's son, John William Norman, followed his dad into the yard when he left school – but kept it quiet from the family. Eventually he ended up as a motor lorry driver – 'nice for me because he used to come to our house for his mid-day dinner, picking me up from Tilton Road School and/or taking me back there from Templefield Street. He was another strong man, having been in a Field Artillery tug-of-war team in World War One. This sport is carried out on horseback.'

A group of railwaymen having a short rest from their work on the 67 ton Sandy Lane Bridge at Bordesley on the Great Western Railway line. Thanks to Mr McPherson.

Old Dick Hockaday was the farrier, the man who shoed the horses, at Lawley Street. He was a shopman, as was his son-in-law, George Carter, who points out that such men are never mentioned. As George stresses, railway shopmen were technically skilled men, such as electricians, engineers, plumbers and fitters of different grades. When George went on the railway 'we started work at Rugby Sheds. These were the steam sheds. Now everybody is fascinated with steam engines, what marvellous things they were. They were very nice things to see when they were running on the railway track but if you ever got into those sheds, especially on a Sunday, they would choke you to death when they was trying to light up.'

George recounts that whatever steel work you put into those sheds went rusty 'and if you touched it with your bare hands you had a brown stain. When I first went on the railway which was 1953 . . . we had to put in the lighting. Now all the conduits for the lighting had to be wrapped up in a special tape which was called Denso and Densalt. Now this tape – the one was a greasy tape which you put on first and then you had to put on the Densalt which was a bituminous tape and had to be put on with a blow lamp. and if you wasn't careful you got scalded.'

Railway shopmen were very skilled men but they were never really classified as railwaymen when it came to talking about wage increases because the railway company always said, 'You're not railwaymen. You're only shopmen.' As a result, 'we came under a different rate of pay, different conditions of service, and do you know whilst our good friends, the locomen, the shunters, the drivers – they all had uniforms provided. We didn't. And it was only in the latter years that we had a set of overalls provided for us. We even had to buy our own tools and again, while I was on the railway, we managed to get that changed.'

Soon after Rugby Sheds, George was moved to Lawley Street to the Outdoor Machinery Department. With his mates he used to go all over the Midlands Area looking at machinery and installing machinery and a lot of the outlying stations were still lit by paraffin and hadn't even got gas. He remembers that they were sent to Washwood Heath to light the sidings and 'we used to have 32 foot poles which were the same as telegraph poles. We used to have to dig a hole in the ground five foot deep and we had to manhandle these poles up into the air, put all the wiring on them. And *it was hard work and we never got no overtime in those days . . . Now you fetch a pole boring machine in. He lifts the pole, drops it into the hole and that's it.'*

George also wants recognition for the cleaners, such as those at the carriage sidings at Vauxhall. Men and women used to clean the carriages and 'they used to release the loos and the filth and the excrement that was all in between the track, in the pits. And it used to smell to the high heavens. Yet they had to clean it all away. And they were poorly paid for the job that they done. When the wind blew through the sheds it was like a gale. But still they carried on. And they got those trains ready for the next day to go out.' Despite such harsh conditions, George emphasises that the cleaners and shopmen were all dedicated to their work and what made things worthwhile were the comradeship and the belief that they were doing a job well.

In 1904 and at the age of twenty, Margaret Smith's grandfather left the Warwickshire village of Claverdon and his job as a farm labourer. He had decided that he was going to head off to Liverpool and emigrate to Canada to join his oldest brother. Arriving in Birmingham, he stopped for a while to earn some money to pay for his voyage. He got a job as a carter for the Great Western Railway and found lodgings with a widow who had a seventeen year old daughter: 'Granddad never got further than Aston! He and my grandmother married and raised a family of thirteen in a back house between Ansell's Brewery and the HP Sauce factory. A far cry from the prairies of Saskatchewan.

As a carter he had to load up the goods that came to Birmingham by train and then deliver them around the city. Margaret recalls that he told her that 'the lead that was to be used for the clock tower at Birmingham University was so heavy that several teams had to be hitched to the wagon'. Each year, he and other railway workers were given two uniform suits but 'Granddad made do with one suit so the other could be altered to fit whichever son was most in need'.

Charles Carolus Abbis also started on the railways as a carter in 1904 – for the old LNWR, later the LMS, and 'all the years my father worked for the railway he always referred to its as the "Company", which he was to dedicate his life to. His working life began at Curzon Street Goods Yard, just down from where he lived in Bartholomew Street in the Italian Quarter – although he brought his own family up nearby in Howe Street.

His son, John, remembers that 'my father had a "knack" with horses and he was called upon many a time by stable men, maybe at night: "Charlie could you come and have a look at a certain horse that doesn't seem to be too good?' Dad's reply, "Give me a couple of minutes to put me boots on", and he would go round to see what he could do'. Early in his career, Charlie had driven lorries with solid tyres but he would say, 'You cannot talk to a piece of iron'. No, he loved the company of a living animal and he loved the annual horse parades that took place in May. W. Crowley was born in Lawley Street, next door to the 'Midland Tavern', and across from the railway stables of the railway and on May Day 'we loved to see the horses. They made a grand sight.'

Mrs S. H. O'Neill has sent me a copy of the notice referring to her grandfather's retirement which appeared in the old Birmingham Gazette. He was George Osbourne and had come to Brum from Cumberworth, Lincolnshire. He did 40 years at Curzon Street LMS depot 'and will be remembered by his colleagues in the goods and cartage departments not only for his cheerful devotion to duty, but also for his unflagging efforts as a Trade Union representative'. He was not sorry that he was retiring as now he could spend more time in his garden.

Sylvia Selfe is a member of a wonderful society, the Birmingham and Midland Society for Genealogy and History, and through her research into her own family history she discovered that her grandfather, Alfred, had been killed in an accident at work in 1904. From Great Alne, near Henley in Arden, he was a carrier at Curzon Street and on the afternoon of his death he had returned to reload his wagon when a pair of horses spooked. Alfred stepped in front of them to calm them down, but because the cart was empty there was no ballast to steady them and they trampled him. Sadly, he lost consciousness and died in the General.

more who did not ride the trains themselves. Then there were the men who helped to shift the goods which were sent across the country on the railways. In Brum, they came in to Lawley Street, Curzon Street, Moor Street, Hockley and other yards, where blokes unloaded them and put them on to wagons which carters drove to destinations all over the place.

This is a cracking shot of Bill Walker who was the last inspector for the GWR when Snow Hill closed as a main line station in 1967. The son of a plate layer, a man who made the railway lines, Bill Walker was one of those many men who devoted their lives to the railways and who ensured that trains ran on time, that stations were clean and that the rail network operated efficiently and effectively. He started as a van lad in the parcels department in 1923, at a time when supposedly light parcels were carried in high carts – but Bill recalls that many of the parcels actually were up to a hundredweight. Five years later, he became a porter at the Bordesley Station and he remembers clearly two nearby shops. These were the coffee house of Joe Bradford, the former goalie with the Blues, who put his footballing medals in the window, and the sweet shop of Joe Fox, who placed his boxing mementoes in his window.

Bill Walker went on to become a goods guard and finally rose to the position of inspector. This shot was taken on March 4, 1967 on platform 7 and the train was the last which was run as a special by the Stephenson Locomotive Society. The engine was the 'Clun Castle', which now is at the museum of steam trains at Tyseley. As the photo was about to be taken by Mr Winckley of the Society, the kids on the platform were annoying the driver – so to shift them, he opened up the cocks to let out some steam. After Snow Hill closed, Bill moved to New Street and retired in 1971.

Despite their different jobs and varying rates of pay, the distinctiveness of the railwaymen was made more pronounced because so many of them lived in certain parts of the city. Tyseley was noted as one such neighbourhood, and came to be associated with a significant proportion of Welsh railwaymen. Then there was Saltley and Alum Rock and the Inkerman Street locality of Nechells.

This clustering came about because the terms of employment of drivers and firemen required them to live within two miles of the depot out of which they worked. To ensure that they woke up in time, the companies paid young lads to act as knockers up. They would traipse about with a long pole and tap on the front bedroom window.

Noted for their trade unionism, railwaymen were prominent in the origins and growth of the Labour party in Birmingham – the strongholds of which were always railway areas. And it was railwaymen who opened the first successful co-operative shop in Brum on the Vauxhall Road. Like the steam trains which brought them into being, the railwaymen of Old Brum impressed themselves upon our city.

King of the Skies: Spitfires

That mid-September day in 1940, hundreds upon hundreds of Brummies had made their way expectantly to the top end of Broad Street, close to the junction with Easy Row. There, opposite the main building of the Municipal Bank, they formed an orderly yet excited square of folk in front of Baskerville House. In the midst of them, and upon the grass, was parked a Messerschmitt which had been brought down over Sussex during the Battle of Britain. It was strange to see such a destructive machine close up. Here was one of that host of war planes which had been unleashed by Hitler to overwhelm British independence and doggedness. No longer frightening, the Messerschmitt drew eyes that were curious. Indeed it had been on show for that

Women and men workers preparing to set to on the fuselages of Spitfires at the Castle Bromwich Spitfire factory.

Ena Field worked as a skin fitter on the starboard wings of Spitfires in 'C' Block of the Castle Bromwich factory: 'it was very new to me, to use an airgun, and different sizes of drills and clippers. It was quite an experience!' Ena had to train for six weeks before she was accepted in the pool 'as we worked on piecework'. Teams of five worked on each part of the wing and with Ena there were Nancy, Bert, Ray and Reg: 'we made many friends. The people we worked with were super.'

W. E. Perks was an electrician's mate at the Castle Bromwich Spitfire Factory from March 1938. He witnessed the first delivery of wing jigs from the Vickers Supermarine factory at Southampton and their installation in 'F' block. He saw Harry Hibs, the noted Blues goalkeeper, and Kid Berg, the famous boxer, operating capstan lathes. Later, working on 'A' Block, Mr Perks watched Hawker Hart aircraft from the Castle Bromwich '605 Squadron' make an emergency landing on the pathway from the Chester Road to the 'Fort Dunlop'. During the war itself, a German plane came out of the clouds in daylight and dropped two oil bombs over the temporary hangar which was used to finish off the completed Spitfires.

Finished planes awaiting to be tested at the Castle Bromwich Spitfire factory.

Now living in Dorset, Don Vickrage was employed as a snagger on the Spitfires and on one occasion Alex Henshaw had detected a popple in the skin between frame numbers fourteen and fifteen on a Spitfire. Sent to sort out the problem, Don worked his way through the AC door and negotiated himself past about ten control cables. Without realising the situation and thinking that the job was done, Alex jumped back into the cockpit to take the Spitfire for its second test flight. He found the controls a bit heavy and shouted to find out what was wrong. Don was still in the fuselage!

All the way from Melbourne, Australia, Mr I. A. Miller has powerful memories of when he was eleven, and Alex Henshaw was his hero. Living about a mile away from the factory, he and his mates would race over to the Castle Bromwich aerodrome so soon as ever they heard the droning of engines which indicated that Alex was about to put another Spitfire through its paces: 'the way that he could make that machine talk, it was like man and machine was one. If there was any pleasure in the war years, it was watching Alex – it was like a private airshow to a boy of 11. To me it was an act of faith or providence that he was there, changing the fate of the war.'

Phyllis Dickinson worked at the Spitfire factory and notes that 'we did a fortnight nights and a fortnight days. The night shift was from 7 p.m. until 7 a.m including Sunday but the friendship and spirit of the workers there made it all worthwhile.'

purpose, to attract people to support the Lord Mayor's Spitfire Fund. This aimed to raise money for the building of British war planes which were so vital in countering the threat from the Luftwaffe, and so quickly was the importance of the fund realised that children from Golden Hillock School collected £75 through their own efforts.

And what better way was there to emphasise the success of the Spitfire in combating the force of the Nazi war machine than to have such a plane fly spectacularly and triumphantly over the unmanned and prone Messerschmitt below? And who better was there to pilot that Spitfire than the great Alex Henshaw himself? A renowned peacetime pilot, Alex was the chief test pilot at the Castle Bromwich Spitfire Factory. In the air above Baskerville House, he performed a low-level 'Victory Roll' – a feat which pulled the crowd into cries of defiance, hope and admiration.

The famed chief test pilot at the Castle Bromwich Spitfire Factory, Alex Henshaw is here piloting a Mark 21 Spitfire.

Michael Middleton of Yardley sent a copy of this article on Spitfire production to Alex Henshaw, the famed pilot who tested the fighter planes made a Castle Bromwich. This was because Alex himself bought a house in Hampton in Arden so that he could be near the Spitfire factory and Michael's family were bred and born there. Indeed, in his book **Sigh for a Merlin**, *Alex refers 'to a Mrs Whitehead the daily help' who is related to Michael by marriage. Following this correspondence, Alex kindly wrote to me about the importance of passing on to younger generations the sacrifices made during the war by the men and women of Brum and the Black Country.*

He states that 'I have always been extremely proud to have been associated with them and like to think that I have more loyal friends in the Midlands than anywhere else'. According to Alex 'the real truth concerning those traumatic years, of Castle Bromwich in particular, will never be fully known'. This is because immediately after the war the Air Ministry instructed the remaining management of the Castle Bromwich Spitfire Factory to destroy all films, negatives and prints in case they fell into enemy hands. Alex stresses that "there were times during the war when ordinary men and women were working under conditions no worse than they had been in the front firing line. I remember them then and I think of them now as the British at their best.'

Without the loyalty, support and dedication of all the Spitfire workers, often under appalling conditions, Alex feels that 'no way could I have maintained the flow of aircraft and the standards by which they were delivered to the fighting squadrons'. Alex, just as you relied upon every single man and woman that worked alongside you, so too did we of a younger generation rely upon all of you for our freedom.

In the hard days of the autumn of 1940, the elan, verve and self confidence of Alex Henshaw was a potent symbol of British defiance. And it was the Spitfires which played a crucial part in giving us the chance to hurl back the Nazi aggressors. As early as 1935 the Government had decided to fund the building of shadow factories for the military aircraft industry. They were to be managed by major motor vehicle firms.

Unsurprisingly, such factories were centred on the West Midlands. In Birmingham itself, the Rover made parts for the Bristol Hercules engine at South Yardley and Solihull, whilst a new factory close to the Austin – its shadow – turned out Fairy Battles, Hurricanes, Stirlings and Lancasters as well as Mercury and Pegasus engines.

The third company operating as a major aircraft factory was the Morris. As part of the Nuffield Organisation, this motor manufacturer constructed a new plant covering 345 acres at Castle Bromwich. From May 1940, the operation was managed by Vickers. Four years later, its workers were making 320 Spitfires and 20 Lancasters a month – more aircraft than any other factory in the United Kingdom. Indeed, throughout the war the men and women of the Castle Bromwich factory produced over 11,000 Spitfires and 300 Lancasters.

Thankfully, the Nazis failed to obliterate the shadow aircraft factories and thankfully their workers ensured that they supplied the planes which ensured that our air force was not knocked out and was victorious. We should never forget that. Nor should we forget the contribution of that fearless and inspirational Spitfire test pilot, Alex Henshaw.

Chapter 5:

Sights, Sounds and Smells
of Old Brum

Holtes on the Hill: Aston Hall

Sir Thomas Holte was a wealthy and powerful man. Well read, versed in several languages and knowledgeable in the law from his time at the Inns of Court, he was one of the biggest and most prominent landowners in the Birmingham region and also had a home in London. Yet for all his intelligence and prosperity, his name was blackened by his reputation for having a vile temper which led him to violence. In particular, it is said that his hand was bloodied by the murder of one of his servants. According to old

A sketch of the grounds of Aston Hall in the 1840s.

Living in Aston, Bill Drew often visited Aston Hall but his most vivid memories are of seeing the building in candlelight. It was an enchanting experience and 'visions of its colourful past came to mind' – although Bill feels that the original builder, Sir Thomas Holte, 'would frown, I'm sure' at the nearby Aston Expressway!' Margaret Manning was well acquainted with Aston Hall because her father, James Higginbotham, was the curator there. For four years from January 1947, the family lived in the North Lodge and then moved into the hall itself – the left-hand side as you look at the place – at the same time as electricity was put in. Margaret left Aston Hall when she married in 1956.

stories, the only person who received a tender word from Sir Thomas was his cook, John, for he 'had found the only way, To reach his master's heart, Was via his esophagus, And ably plied his art'.

Then one day, Sir Thomas was out hunting deer when one of his companions, Richard Smallbroke, wagered his swiftest horse that if they rode back unexpectedly to Holte's home they would find his cook unprepared. Sir Thomas accepted the bet with alacrity, declaring 'I'd sooner doubt the sun, To keep his accustomed time, Than doubt my good cook John'. Unhappily, when the hunting party arrived at Duddeston Hall, where the Holtes then lived, the table was unspread. Enraged because he had lost the wager and had been shown up, Sir Thomas 'seized a cleaver keen and cold' and cleft the skull of his cook in twain. The story may well be based on truth, for in 1606, Sir Thomas sued for slander a William Ascrick of Birmingham, who had recounted the tale. Awarded just £30 damages, Sir Thomas lost even this when the verdict was overturned on appeal.

Still, the rumours of murder did not stop Sir Thomas from rising socially and in 1611, he paid the great sum of £1095 to buy a baronetcy. The money raised supposedly was to have gone towards the cost of the British army in Ulster. This is reckoned to explain the fact that the red hand of Ulster was taken as the Holte's coat of arms, although less kindly folk proposed that in reality it signified the bloody hand of Sir Thomas. Keen to flaunt his new status and power locally, Sir Thomas decided to build a new home on a hill overlooking Aston Church. This prominent position would allow him to look across his wide lands, which included Duddeston and Nechells as well as Aston, and to proclaim to the world his success and significance.

Sir Thomas paid John Thorpe, a well-respected land surveyor, to design his house and then engaged masons, carpenters and other craftsmen to build it. The foundations were made of big bands of iron slag, most of which probably came from the Aston Furnace which was to give its name to Furnace Lane in Lozells. Similarly, the bricks for the shell of the hall were made from local clay and were dressed with soft grey sandstone. The rest of the house was made of timber and for this purpose, several hundred oak trees were cut down on the Holte estates.

Work on Aston Hall began in 1618 and Sir Thomas was able to move his home there in May 1631, although construction was not completed for at least another four years. It was a spectacular building and amongst its rooms on the ground floor were a Great Hall (now the Entrance Hall), a Great Parlour in which Sir Thomas dined, and kitchens.

A superb cantilevered oak staircase ran round a square well up to the floors above. On the first was the Great Dining Room; the Best Lodging Chamber, where King Charles I slept on October 18, 1642; the Withdrawing Room; and the Long Gallery. Originally this was about 125 feet long and was used for a variety of purposes, such as for music and pictures. Up on the second floor is where the servants slept and here is to be found 'Dick's Garrett', a low attic which was called this name from at least the later 1700s.

Mr Dewson was the chief keeper of Aston Hall and here on December 6, 1949 he is in the Long Gallery examining the seventeenth century writing desk used by Charles 1.

Edna Burbridge, nee Emberton, recalls going to Aston Hall in the 1920s on a trip with Guildford Street Girls School. The children were taken up to 'Dick's Garrett', where a piece of old rope was attached to the centre beam and from which Dick, a servant of the Holtes, was supposed to have hung himself. Edna also remembers that they were told that Thomas Holte had imprisoned his daughter above the kitchen to make her give up the thought of marrying her lover of whom her father disapproved. Stubbornly she refused and it is said that she died there.

Ms A. Dunshee is another person who grew up locally and recollects the Russian Cossacks with their horses. They used to charge up the long and wide drive of Aston Hall and stable their animals at the back of the toilets. Ms Dunshee also has tales of tunnels: 'under the stairs was a door and hanging from the door was a chair. When the door was open, there was a passage which led to Aston Church. It was a secret place for people to hide from Cromwell's soldiers.'

During the English Civil War, Sir Thomas was a lukewarm Royalist, but even so Aston Hall was attacked by Parliamentarians from Birmingham in 1643. After a three-day siege and bombardments which damaged the balustrade of the Great Stairs, Sir Thomas surrendered.

Sir Thomas died in 1654, by which time he was also the lord of Erdington and Pype. His descendants lived at Aston Hall until 1770. The male line of the family died out soon after, and the building came into the possession of Heneage Legge and later James Watt, the son of the great engineer. It was taken over by Birmingham City Council in 1864. Today Aston Hall is one of the finest Jacobean mansions in England and calls out the bond between a major urban centre and its rural past.

A gardener working on one of the fine floral displays in Aston Park on August 3, 1951. This feature in the foreground of Aston Hall had 4,000 blooms.

Sylvia Rushton, nee Mason, lived close to Aston Hall at 1 back of 215, Park Lane and can't bring to mind 'ever seeing a blade of grass let alone flowers in our yard. So it was wonderful for me and my sisters, Jeannette and Barbara, to go to Aston Park'. They took with them their jam sandwiches and bottle of water and after eating and drinking would sneak in with the visitors into Aston Hall. The girls were fascinated by the stories told by the guides and 'would wonder in amazement at the holes made by the cannon balls during the Civil War, but most of all us kids loved the secret passage'. Elizabeth Cooper, nee Thay, came from Stuart Street, Nechells and her mother used to urge her and her four younger sisters 'never to forget that our ancestral home was Aston Hall and also that an underground passage ran from "The Old Ladies Park" in Elliot Street, Nechells to Aston Hall, although she never told us how she gained that knowledge'.

Now living in Greece, Janet Fownes has wonderful memories of Aston Hall as once she lived in Aston Park as her father is William Gurney – one of the park's former gardeners. The family moved into one of the lodges on the main gate when Janet was one in 1947 and they stayed there for twelve years. Amongst the other gardeners were Danky, Ginger Palmer, Godfrey Lavander and Norman Mellor, whilst Janet also brings to mind others attached to the Hall – such as the Higginbottoms, the Healeys and their son Roger, Mr and Mrs Davis (the Superintendant) and daughter Barbara and Mr and Mrs Phillips and daughter Barbara, 'whom I used to play with'.

One from the Vaults: The BAI

The 1830s and 1840s were turbulent times marked by economic hardships, political disturbances and a mass migration of people. Hundreds of thousands of folk abandoned the countryside and in search of work, hope and excitement they poured into the expanding industrial towns of England, Wales and Scotland. This movement forced the towns to grab nearby fields and overlay them with buildings and criss-cross them with streets, cuts and railway lines. And as these land hungry towns stretched ever outwards, open spaces within them were swallowed up. Where so many were packed into so tight an area, there was so little room for physical recreation.

In these circumstances, many wealthy folk feared that the British would no longer be fit enough for the nation to continue as a major power. Thus preoccupied, a number of better-off Brummies founded the Athenic Institute in Suffolk Street in 1841. Targeting working-class men, it aimed to provide members 'with the means by which may be obtained mental, moral and physical improvement, together with rational amusement.'

Little else is known about the Institute, but in 1866 it was followed by the better-recorded Birmingham Athletic Club. Begun by young chaps who were interested in gymnastics, athletics and other physical activities, it was based at a room in the poultry bay of Bingley Hall – although the club also had athletic grounds in Portland Road, Rotton Park and used Kent Street Swimming Baths.

Within a few years, the BAC had gained a fine reputation nationally as a pioneer in the field of physical education. One of its members was George Dixon, a politician who was passionate about education and who campaigned vigorously for physical exercise to be included in the curriculum of schools. He achieved his goal locally in 1886, and the town's example was soon followed by Sheffield, Leeds and other places.

However, the need for a nation of healthy workers and fit soldiers was still paramount in the thoughts of many proponents of physical education, as was made plain by Lord Beresford MP in a speech in Birmingham in 1888. The inaugural president of the National Physical Recreation Society, he declared that 'never in the history of the empire was it more needful or more important that the people of England should be encouraged to pursue every sort of manual sport and exercise'.

Praising the Birmingham Athletic Club, Lord Beresford emphasised how the club was disadvantaged because it had to move three or four times a year for other functions. He urged the town to remedy this problem by providing a piece of land 'whereon a gymnasium, not for 300, but for 3,000 might be built'.

Spurred on by this call, the Birmingham Athletic Club launched a fund to provide a civic gymnasium for the citizens of Brum. Swiftly, though, it was drawn instead into supporting the proposals of two of its members – George Kenrick of the famous manufacturing family, and Dr A. H. Carter, senior physician to the Queen's Hospital.

The first women's head of the Birmingham Athletic Institute was Mrs Eileen Harper and here she is leading a ladies afternoon keep fit class in 1937.

Pauline Cubbins was one of those many thousands of folk who were attracted by the variety of activities offered at the BAI. In 1963/64 she was a Civil Servant and along with her workmate, Diane, she decided to join a Keep Fit class at the BAI. Diane pulled a calf muscle in the first two sessions, 'but we persevered. As a result, when the BAI was approached to provide 20 young, fit people to go on a skiing holiday we volunteered with enthusiasm. It was part of an interchange with young people from Frankfurt, Lyons and Birmingham.' The event took place in Germany and 'we had a fantastic time – yes we did learn to ski after a fashion'. The trip developed in Diane a love of skiing and apart from two years, she has gone skiing every year since – 'so thank you BAI for giving me the opportunity'.

Joan Seabourne also recalls going to keep fit classes at the BAI. In her case they were done to music and as a pianist played, a teacher called out the moves. Later Joan took part in national dancing and Scottish dancing. When she first went to the BAI in the 1950s the place had a green uniform which you could buy. Later on the uniform could be bought in blue. For women, these consisted of a tunic and matching knickers and Joan still has hers.

Marguerite Marsh was fourteen when she joined the BAI at Severn Street in 1940-41. A couple of years later she took a training course to teach keep fit to adults. This was run by the City's Education Department in conjunction with the BAI. The training took place in term time each Saturday afternoon at Metchley Lane Playing Fields and it went on for two years – and 'we also had to attend classes at the BAI at least once a week'. Marguerite later trained at the BAI in John Bright Street and when that was closed 'we were moved into premises adjacent to the Hippodrome and our Wednesday day class still continued. Now the name has changed again and it is now Dance Xchange, yet we still have our keep fit classes. Many of us are old BAI ladies but since the closure of the Hip we meet at the MAC in Cannon Hill Park.'

Margaret Harris, nee George, was a member of the Girls Life Brigade – now just the Girls Brigade – attached to the 45th Birmingham Company at Kings Norton Methodist Church. They had their own company displays but for special occasions for Birmingham Divisional Displays 'we joined with the companies from Selly Park Baptists and the Congregational Church in Cotteridge'. On one of these occasions, 'we were trained at the BAI in Metchley Lane for a very intricate skipping ballet! Then in June 1948 we performed three national dances at the London International Rally in the Central Hall at Westminster. We were instructed at these in Metchley Lane over several weeks, because they were dances with very complex steps.'

A gymnastic display at the Birmingham and Midland Institute in 1956. Thanks to Bernard Thomas.

For many years, Bernard Thomas was a key figure in the Birmingham Athletic Institute and stresses that the BAI 'was unique in that it was the first institute in the country to devote time, space, and indeed money, to physical recreation'. Many of the top international gymnasts also came from Birmingham, amongst them great names such as 'Walter Tysull in the late 19th century, and "Pop" Bradley. "Pop" was very well known in the area, as he taught not only at the BAI, but also at Five Ways Grammar School, the YMCA, and later in Sutton Coldfield. He brought along other flourishing gymnasts of international repute, such as Harry Finchett, and he was indeed one of my early coaches.' As a noted gymnast and teacher himself, Bernard is proud that the 'BAI gym club was the first civilian gym club in post-war days to beat the Army – no mean feat as the Army team consisted entirely of members of the Army PT School staff, and, without wishing to be biased, could be considered almost professionals'. Bernard also points out the BAI was very much a multi-disciplinary institute, that there was hardly any indoor sport which was not included, and that during the Second World War and for a short time afterwards, Birmingham's major parks were the venues for plays, performances by bands, and displays of all kinds.

G. F. King was a keen member of the BAI and he stresses that 'at the BAI there were some of the finest gymnasts in the country being trained by Bernard Thomas before he became the England physio'. John E. Graeme Edwards is an original member of the BAI and although he gave instructions in tennis, his biggest interest, 'as a pre-war skier, was in the formation of the BAI Ski Club, which became a major activity. I arranged dry ski-ing classes, followed by a ski holiday abroad . . . For the original holidays a train carriage was hired from Birmingham to Paris, and a French carriage for travel onward. This latter was a basic open space with a bar, and the night was spent in dancing.' After marriage, John reduced his connection with ski-ing but the club continued to thrive under the guidance of Harold Ward.

They proposed the foundation of the Birmingham Athletic Institute to provide a large, fully equipped and central gymnasium; four or more branch gymnasiums in hired rooms; and a staff of instructors. The BAI would also encourage the formation of clubs for boys and girls in schools and would push forward 'healthy and desirable forms of physical exercise and recreation, by lectures, displays etc.'.

Paid for by George Kenrick, a new gymnasium was erected in John Bright Street. Soon after, the Birmingham School Board transferred the responsibilities of its

Physical Exercises Committee to the BAI and benefactors leased 29 acres of land off the Pershore Road for playing fields.

Opened officially in February 1892, the BAI came to have a major impact on the life of Birmingham and on the health of its people and from 1917, it was brought into the municipal sphere when its John Bright Street building was given to the City's Education Committee. This body continued to supervise the BAI until 1984 when it became part of the City's Recreation and Community Services Department – by which date the BAI was based at new premises in Balsall Heath.

The BAI could never have arisen nor could it have carried on its important work if it had not been for the beliefs in civic responsibility, civic institutions and municipal activity. The significance of all can be forgotten too easily. They should not be.

This photo shows John Castle skipping in his suit for publicity for a special Businessmen's Keep Fit Class. He had first gone to the BAI as a small boy in 1924 when, because he had some breathing difficulties, a friend of the family used to take him to Severn Street – but 'I can only remember lying on the floor and taking deep breaths'. Later, when John came out of the army in 1946, several of his friends invited him to join a Friday night class that was called Recreational Keep Fit and Games. He kept this up for several years and then changed over to the Businessmen's Keep Fit Class on Tuesday nights. This was taken by Eric Bates 'who was absolutely marvellous and got the extra ounce of energy out of us'.

John's wife, Dorothy, also attended the BAI. During the early years of the Second World War, she was training to be a teacher at college in Edmund Street and after her lectures she would go to the ballet class. This was taken by 'a very enthusiastic lady, Miss Waterman, whose slim straight-up-and-down figure was perfect for all contortions. I remembered she despaired of our arabesques etc. "These girls have all got hips", she moaned. A real character who lived for ballet . . . Unfortunately, I still have hips!'

Skid Kids: Cycle Speedway

It was all they wanted to do, be like their heroes in the Birmingham Speedway team. Each Saturday they made their way enthusiastically over to Perry Barr to watch Geoff Bennett, Graham Warren, the 'Blonde Bombshell', and others tearing around the track, spurting wells of cinder into the air and amazingly hanging on as they took bends at speed with one leg trailing behind them.

But these speedway fans weren't daft. They knew there was fat chance of any of them ever becoming stars and so instead of kicking their heels and moaning and groaning about their lot they did the next best thing – they became the 'skid kids' of cycle speedway.

First, though, they had to get a track. That wornt too much of a problem because in the Brum of 1946 there were plenty of bomb pecks about that could be sorted out and turned into something special. And that's what they did.

Night after night dozens of them scoured over one of the many local sites wasted by German bombers. They cleared as much of a space as they could, shifting bricks, bits of wood and debris until they had as flattish a piece of land as they could get. Then they grabbed hold of the bricks and laid them out laboriously until the shape of a track came into full view. That done, they fetched bag after bag of cinders and emptied them so that a black oval racing track could emerge.

With their track almost ready, the lads turned away from collective action and focused upon their individual needs – to get a bike ready for racing. With distinctive cow-horn handle bars, each cycle was stripped down of its bell, cycle pumps and anything else that could get in the way of maximising the chance of as much speed as was possible from a light and unhindered frame.

That first night when everything was set, they looked around and were dead chuffed with theirselves. Casting their young eyes over their hard-won achievement they realised that they weren't on their own for a bit of a crowd had gathered. There must have been 300 or 400 people at the track. Many of them were young girls who'd come to see their boyfriends but a lot were older folk who were pleased to see youngsters doing something for themselves and having a go.

Quickly, it was time for the first four riders to come to the starting line and so soon as ever the signal was given they were off! They had no fancy footwear and nothing to protect them from a knock if they come a purler – but that never bothered them. For each of them was filled with the thrill of the race, the excitement of going as fast as they could and the desire to be the first winner of all. And what did it matter if they ended up bruised and scraged? Not at all to them as youthful as they were in their strength and vitality.

From its beginnings with the Birmingham Tigers at their bomb peck in Sparkhill in 1946, cycle speedway raced across Brummagem. There were the Erdington Pirates, Yardley Wood Aces, Bromford Crusaders, Glebe Panthers, Handsworth Hornets, Oscott Hammers, Perry Barr Juniors, Quinton Racers, Sheldon Boomerangs, Warren

Hill Rangers, Sutton Stars, Hall Green Hurricanes, Hockley Flyers, Elmdon Bees, Shirley Cyclones, Bordesley Green Aces, Wythall Whippets, and the Aston Aces run by the well-respected Mr and Mrs Robinson.

That's not to forget the Birmingham Lions. With a track on the Balsall Heath Road, the Lions speeded about under makeshift floodlights guided by their manager Fred Goode. Then, of course, there were the Kingstanding Monarchs. Formed in 1948 with Harold Smith as a leading light, they entered the second division of the Birmingham and District Cycle Speedway League which had been set up through the work of speedway promoter Les Marshall and Supporters' Club secretary, Mrs Cooper.

The crowds have gathered here in 1951 at the cycle speedway track between Alfred Road, the Stoney Lane and Beech Road, Sparkhill that was the home of the Birmingham Tigers. The Brummie lads are set to take on the Kingsdown Aces of Swindon and they're represented by Taffy Hill, second from the left, and Basil Wainwright, nearest to the camera. Thanks to Taffy Hill, one of the original members of the Tigers who went on to ride for the Birmingham Lions and for Wales.

Born in 1941, Tony Robbins lived in Park Road near to The Flat and 'as kids we used to play around the local streets and one place we went to was an alley up Key Hill opposite Key Hill Drive behind the Post Office. Down this alley was a piece of waste ground which seemed to be a huge crater in the middle of which was a circular path worn away by the many bikes that used to be raced around it on a Sunday afternoon.' There was a starting gate, a long length of orange rubber 'which was stretched across the track and all the bike racers lined up waiting for the start. Someone would release the rubber band and they were off. The bikes had thick treaded tyres and cow horn handles with no brakes.' Tony remembers that the races were organised by fourteen-year old Graham Hancox who lived in Ford Street, down an alley opposite Findon's sweet shop.

The Monarchs soon gained promotion and came to dominate cycle speedway locally. Still by the late 1950s the sport was in decline as bomb sites were built upon and as other activities began to attract young blokes. But cycle speedway did not disappear. After a number of moves, the Birmingham Lions became Sandwell whilst the Kingstanding Monarchs are known now as Birmingham Monarchs. Both clubs carry on the dream of those young fellers who brought cycle speedway to Brum in the late 1940s.

In a race in 1950 that is believed to be the first by a Birmingham team against opposition from outside the Midlands, the Kingstanding Monarchs are speeding against the Stockport Stars. The Monarchs pair are Brian Smith on the inside and John Palmer on the outside and they are squeezing out the Stockport rider in the cap. They went on to give the Monarchs a 5-1 start. Thanks to John Palmer. Like Taffy, John is a Welsh Brummie and he gained a great reputation as a cycle speedway ace and a champion of the Birmingham and District Cycle Speedway League.

Brian O'Kelly was amongst a bunch of lads in Sparkhill, most of whom went to College Road School and who decided to form a cycle speedway tream. Their home track was on a piece of waste land on the corner of Colebank Road and the Startford Road, Hall Green and now the site of a garden near to South Birmingham College. A team manager was appointed, 'my Mom's lodger', and contests were arranged. Brian recalls other tracks such as that at the brickworks on the Warwick Road in Greet, and notes how 'some lads made several alterations to their bikes, others just took the bell off the handlebars and the cycle pump off the frame.

In the early 1950s, Pat Gupwell, nee Long, managed a cycle speedway team called Yardley Eagles which raced on wasteland at Hay Mills. Here she is with her team in 1950. Pat recollects that 'everything was made and organised by the boys. We spent hours painting green eagles on silver tabards. Our starting gate was a strong piece of rubber elastic. There were cycle speedway leagues and our team arrived in the back of a lorry to away games.' Romance blossomed fro Pat at the cycle speedway, for she married the lad on her right and they have been together for 44 years.

    Ray Middleton has strong memories of two tracks in particular: the one was at Bromford Bridge and the other at 'what is now the car park of the Heron's Nest just past Knowle, on the Warwick Road. The tracks were considerably smaller ovals than the motor cycle equivalents but were cinder the same. As far as I can remember no safety equipment was worn so scratches and bruises were commonplace.'

    Cliff Hanchett was one of the skid kids from the age of thirteen in 1946 after his sisters took him to the Alexander Stadium, Perry Barr to see the first Speedway match after the war 'and like so many young lads in thopse days, I was so enthralled by it all. The next day my bike was stripped down – no mudguards, no brakes or lights. We would put sand on the roads to make a skid patch, then we would pedal as fast as our legs would go and then throw the back wheel into a full broadside. By this time cycle speedway had taken off big time. Tracks started to appear on every available piece of ground. This all happened in 1946 and within no time the league was set up consisting of two divisions. the second divisioon the riders were upto 16 years of age and the first division was 16 to 18 years old.'

    Cliff rode for the Oscott Hammers, the Rogues, who won the league in 1949 and whose track was in Old Oscott Lane. The winning medals were presented by the Birmingham Speedway Captain, Stan Dell ' – my hero at the time. The same year I was presented with a cup medal riding for Handsworth Hammers, this time by Graham Warren. The next season I joined Kingstanding Monarchs, finishing with them at the end of the 1953 season.' Cliff brings to mind Harry Robinson and his wife, Mrs Cooper and 'others who set up the sport and the likes of Harold Smith who carried it on wholeheartedly until he died at a young age. Amongst Cliff's teammates at the Monarchs was Tony Rake who had ridden for Erdington Pirates. Tony was mad keen on cycle speedway and he also raced for Aldridge Hammers. He made some great friends during his time as a rider and even met his wife through cycle speedway.

Crowning Glory of Brum: The Old Crown

He was a man with a passion was John Leland. Entrusted by Henry VIII with the power to search for records of antiquity in the cathedrals, colleges, abbeys and priories of England, he became 'totally enflammid with a love to see thoroughly all those partes of this your opulente and ample reaulme'.

One part of that realm visited by Leland was Birmingham and it is to him that we owe the earliest description of our town other than for legal purposes. He came to 'Bremischam' from Norton – now Kings Norton – having crossed a little brook to the east of this 'attractive country town' in Worcestershire and passed through 'good areas of woodland and pasture and reasonably good arable'.

Approaching from the south, Leland 'came through a pretty street, or ever I entred, into Bermingham towne. This street, as I remember, is called Dirtye (Deritend High Street). In it dwell smithes and cutlers, and there is a brooke (the River Rea) that divideth this street from Bermingham, and is an Hamlett, or Membre, belonging to the Parish therebye. There is at the end of Dirtey a propper chappell, and mansion house of tymber, hard on the ripe (bank), as the brooke runneth down . . .'

The chapel was that of Saint John's, Deritend whilst the mansion was what we now call 'The Old Crown' pub. And that description by Leland makes plain why this black and white timber-framed building is so important to all Brummies. For although it has been changed and added to, its historical structure is powerful – for it strikes out deep into our past and bonds us with the time when Brum was a growing market town

A wonderful painting of High Street Deritend by G. Warren Blackham (1870-1900). Thanks to Birmingham Museum and Art Gallery. The painting is a watercolour and is in the City's permanent collection. The Old Crown is on the right and up on the left is Saint John's Church, Deritend which was knocked down in the early twentieth century.

An evocative shot of the 'Old Crown' in December 1938. For many years, the right-hand part of the ground floor of the building was Rodway's Restaurant. It then became a cafe and today that section is included in the present restaurant of the pub.

The grandfather of Shiela T. Skoczylas was George Henry Rodway. After he and his wife died before the First World War, their restaurant was run by their daughter and her younger brother, Cyril and 'when my uncle joined the army my mother carried on until his return. When the premises were being refurbished for this latest venture several things were commented upon in the B'ham Mail, in its early stages of restoration, evidence of horses, a well, and a masonic carving. These are no mysteries to me … Mother said in the days when the farmers drove their cattle into market they would spend some of their gains in the Olde Crowne and get rather typsy; fearing the wrath of their wives they would pop into Rodway's to buy cakes to placate their womenfolk. This is why the shop was open late'.

bustling with traders and manufacturers, preparing to thrust itself on to the world stage as a city of international repute.

All of us Brummies grew up thinking that the 'Old Crown' was built in 1368 – for has not that fact been proclaimed for generations in bold letters outside the pub? However, it is more likely that it was erected between 1450 and 1500. The main building material was oak and it is probable that its frame was made and put together on the site.

Whatever the case, certainly the 'Old Crown' was impressive enough for Leland to mention it. Indeed, the only other Birmingham buildings he comments upon are Saint John's and the parish church of Saint Martin's. Then in 1589, we know that 'the deedes of the Crowne House' are mentioned in a document relating to John Dyckson of Birmingham. He was a carrier and given the importance of High Street Deritend as a route into Birmingham it is obvious that the 'Old Crown' must have been a good base for his business.

Originally having only a ground floor of a large central hall around which were smaller rooms, an upper floor was added to the 'Old Crown' in the 1600s. Also in that

Looking up High Street Deritend with the Old Crown dominating the photo in the late 1930s.

Some of George Pemberton's earliest memories are of going with his mom to her job at the 'Old Crown' in the late 1940s. He recalls that 'the place was always teeming with barrow boys and local workers. Joe Fox the boxer used to call in as did some of Birmingham City Football Club. Mom was a well known character called Nell Pemberton, nee Nellie Village, and was from a very popular Small Heath family. Mom also had a job at Haddon and Stoke's and when she collected her wages I got a wage packet too with some farthings in.'

century, in 1673, an Edward Barber is given as the tenant and it is stated that he was using the building as an inn. Within a few years, the 'Old Crown' was split first into two properties and then into three.

Passing through the hands of various owners, by the mid-1800s, the 'Old Crown' had fallen into disrepair and it was a run-down structure. It was then that it was bought by Joshua Toulmin Smith. A devoted inquirer into Birmingham's past, it is doubtful whether the 'Old Crown' would have survived without his dedication and determination. In 1851, Birmingham Corporation included the building in an 'improvement' scheme – intending to knock it down. Toulmin Smith 'successfully resisted that attempt', as he did others in 1856 and 1861.

In his own words, this benefactor to our city explained that 'it is somewhat hard that I should have been obliged, at my own trouble and expense, to save, for the Town, a relic of antiquity which is for the credit and interest of the Town; and certainly not for my personal profit, should be preserved . . .'

Toulmin Smith's words echo strongly today. In the later twentieth century, the 'Old Crown' once again required major restoration work if it were to be passed on to future generations of Brummies. And once again a big-hearted family took up the cause, for that essential work has been carried out by the Brennans at a huge cost to themselves. An Irish Brummie family, they resolved to breathe new life into the 'Old Crown' through respecting its past. At their own expense and with no support they have given back to us the people of Birmingham one of the most vital and important buildings in our city. We owe them a great debt of gratitude.

Sunk Without Trace: The River Rea

Brum is unique amongst the great cities of the world. It has no over-riding natural, physical or geographical advantages to explain its emergence and development in to a settlement of international repute. Birmingham certainly isn't a defensive site. We might have Weoley Castle but not even the most ardent Brummie could pretend that its meagre ruins are in the same league as the mighty fortress of Edinburgh. Neither is our city a major port. We might boast of Gas Street Basin and Saltley Docks, but even the most fervent of us could never suggest that we have bays to compare with that of Dublin or channels to equal that of Bristol.

Nor is Brum on the banks of a wide and fast river. We have nothing to equal the Seine of Paris, the Danube of Vienna, the Nile of Cairo and the Rhine of Rotterdam. Birmingham waters are short and narrow, and yet they should not be dismissed too easily. They might be small but they have played an important part in our history. Like the Spark Brook, some were main boundaries, whilst others such as the Bourn Brook, Hol Brook and Wash Brook powered mills of every kind. But foremost amongst the water courses of Brum was the Rea. Its name comes from the Anglo-Saxon words 'atter e' – which actually means 'att the river'.

Rising in the Lickey Hills it flows north east towards Saltley. In the Middle Ages it was forded most easily between Digbeth and Deritend. This spot was the meeting place of routes from Coventry, Warwick and Stratford to the east and Worcester, Dudley, Wolverhampton and Shrewsbury to the west. Birmingham began on the slopes of this important crossing point, whilst along the banks of the Rea there were significant buildings like Heath Mill – where edge tools, swords and cutlery were ground.

Despite the presence of blade mills, as late as 1800 the Rea was described as 'a nice, clear stream, always full of water.' Below Deritend Bridge, where Floodgate Street now is, there were 'pleasant tea gardens' which were 'well wooded down to the river's edge, having pretty walks, grottos and arbours'. Known as Spring Gardens, this rural retreat was popular with people wanting a day out from the town. If you fancied it, you could hire a pleasure boat and row up the Rea, below the Bradford Street and Cheapside bridges, until you came to the secluded and elegant gardens of the Apollo Hotel in Moseley Street.

But as Brum grew, so the Rea became polluted with the outpourings of industry and the refuse of an exploding population. By the mid-1800s it had become an open sewer and 'a burial place for unfortunate canines and felines'. The same thing happened to the Hockley Brook, and both flowed unchecked in to the River Tame at Saltley. This is the watershed for almost the whole of Birmingham. It begins in the Black Country and passes through Perry Barr and Saltley before going on to Tamworth and then the River Trent. By the late nineteenth century large sewage works had been constructed close to the Tame at Tyburn Road and main sewers had been built along the lines of the Hockley Brook and the Rea.

A marvellous photo of navvies working on improving the storm water drainage on the River Rea in the city centre in 1893.

Still, all three courses were dark, filthy and liable to break their banks. In the early 1900s there was severe flooding in many places, including Breedon Cross, Cotteridge. Fort Dunlop, Erdington and the Argyle Street neighbourhood of Nechells. The council had no option except to carry out expensive improvements. Between 1917 and 1929, the Hockley brook was lowered and culverted from Perrot Street, Winson Green to Plume Street, Nechells. It was a huge task, the largest in the country, and cost the enormous sum of £758,000. After it was finished, work began on widening and deepening a five mile stretch of the Tame from its juncture with the Rea. Then this river itself was thrust from view when it was pushed down in to the ground all the way from Saltley to Sir John's Road, Selly Park. One river has not been hidden and lost. The Cole still flows at ground level from Solihull, through Yardley Wood and Hall Green, and along the edges of Sparkhill, Greet, Tyseley, Hay Mills, Small Heath and Stechford until it leaves Brum at Sheldon. Perhaps it's time to raise the Rea back in to sight and to let folk walk along its banks – as once they did in Old Brum.

Onlookers at the spot where a German bombing had shattered the banks of the River Rea at Gooch Street, April 12, 1941.

Youngsters watching the swollen River Rea at Lifford in April 1977. Thanks to the **Birmingham Evening Mail**.

Settlement of Hope: The Summer Lane Settlement

It was the biggest paradox of the age. Victorian Britain had the greatest empire in history. It had the most powerful navy on the seas. It was the wealthiest nation in the world. Yet the riches which poured from its mines, factories and workshops did not reach millions of Britons. For in a land where there was so much affluence, there were so many who were poor. In each town, city and village, men traipsed the streets looking for jobs. Everywhere women scratted to make ends meet by taking in washing and charring. And throughout the country, ragged and barefooted children gathered outside factory gates to plead for scraps of food from those who were lucky enough to have a full time job.

Appalled by so much poverty in the midst of plenty, there were some amongst the middle class who endeavoured to help the poor. Amongst them were a number of Birmingham women who had a marked social conscience. They included Jessie Lloyd and Miss Caswell, the instigators of an infant welfare centre in Floodgate Street. There was Catherine Osler, who worked for children with learning difficulties. And then there was Alice Beal. A Kenrick by birth, she was a pioneer of social work in Brum and was active in setting up the Birmingham Women's Hospital. She believed strongly that members of the middle class owed a duty to those who were less fortunate, feeling that they ought to go and live for a time in a poorer neighbourhood. In this way the better-off could learn about the problems caused by poverty and so seek ways to help the poor.

With Agnes Barrow, Ellen Pinsent and other prominent women, Beale set up a committee to make this idea a reality by establishing a settlement somewhere in Brum. They focused their attention on Summer Lane. Stretching from Alma Street, Aston, to the 'Salutation' at Snow Hill, The Lane had a host of small streets running off it and the whole district was packed with factories, shops and back-to-backs. It had a significant number of lower middle class retailers and regularly employed workers, but many of its folks were in precarious or low-paid jobs and were poor through no fault of their own. They had to live in substandard housing with inadequate facilities, and illness and early deaths were widespread.

These were problems which Alice Beale and her friends wanted to attack. Early in 1899 they took over No 4 Colmore Terrace, a large Georgian house with 'a dilapidated appearance' on the corner of Upper Tower Street and Summer Lane. May Stavely was appointed warden, and she was joined by four resident workers and another seven who lived out. They decided that the main thrust of their actions should be the support and care of women and children. Within a few years the Birmingham Women's Settlement workers and local helpers had established themselves as a major force for good.

Provident collections were organised so that people could save as little as tuppence a week, drawing out the money when they needed it. Widows and the elderly were taken care of. Loans were made both for the purchase of spectacles and medical care. Country holidays were arranged for kids who had never seen fields or cows. And

Women attached to the Birmingham Settlement at its opening on September 29, 1899.

Mrs C. Marsh used to live at 43, Summer Lane. Her family was Jarvis the greengrocer's and her father 'used to supply fruit and vegetables for the visitors etc staying at the Settlement. Indeed I remember the lady I recall as 'Floss' loaning her pushchair to me if the delivery was too heavy for me to carry. I would be about 9-10 yrs of age. We lived at the shop until the bombing in Hospital Street (1940/41) devastated the area. Our premises had all the windows blown out and doors blown off their hinges. The bombing raids were a nightmare but that particular night of the landmine (via parachute) was a dreadful nightmare – I still remember the screams... I also remember the day having to go to work without a wash. The fires the night before had been so severe the water supply in the area was all used up. There were stand-pipes in the street and we were allowed only 1 kettle of water for breakfast.' Mrs Marsh's father's shop had a 'beautiful window display of fruit and vegetables'.

physically disabled children were visited regularly, taken to hospitals, sent on convalescence and brought to 'Happy Evenings' to play in the club room and the garden.

The Settlement was involved in plenty of other activities. A day nursery was established, talks were given, a Poor Man's Lawyer offered his services, and mothers met each other. Nor were teenagers neglected. There was a Girl's Club which had regular meetings and which arranged trips to Woodcock Street Baths and to the homes of the residents in Edgbaston. But the Settlement wasn't just a one-way street. If the

Members of the Summer Lane Settlement's Monday Mothers' Club stepping out to the tune of the 'Lambeth Walk' in 1938.

Alan Davies of Chelmsley Wood met his wife at the Settlement more than 45 years ago – but adds the rush for the boys to get upstairs to the girls' club for the last half-hour owed nothing to romance, instead it was because 'the girls' tennis table was in better nick than ours'. Pauline Mannion recalls the Settlement as a Godsend for children in the poorer areas round it: 'helpers were drawn from wealthier families' and there was a Mr Chinn who was the probation officer who also helped out. So too did Pauline's brother, Bernard, who taught carpentry at the Settlement.

Pauline adds that Jim Oxby was the football coach, while Miss Gateley took the girls for netball and 'when the latter weren't playing, they made dresses for themselves to take on holiday and dancing. I went with the Swedish dancing team and that represented the Settlement at Wembley. There was a library which we all used and the week's highlight was the Saturday night dances, where for 6d, the boys could meet the girls. Every holiday time we went camping for the weekend. Not far perhaps, only locally, but the lorries would roll up to take us to places like Ullenhall. In August came our week away at a self-catering camp or a hostel. Lots of marriages were formed at the Settlement, which I regard as one of the happiest places I've ever visited.'

residents helped and gave advice, then they also learned from the mothers and daughters of Summer Lane about loyalty neighbourliness, determination and the skills needed to wage war against poverty day in and day out.

The Settlement was a beacon of social justice in Old Brum and its workers continued to do good throughout the years of the Depression and during the Second World War. And they continue to do good with sports and out-of-school clubs, with National Vocational Qualification classes for women who want to return to work, with child care, and with a great variety of services for those in debt. As in the past, the Settlement's over-riding aim is clear: to strive for a window of opportunity for everyone. Long may it continue.

Youngsters enjoying a glass of milk at the Summer Lane Settlement in the 1930s.

What memories Charlie Crow has of the Birmingham Settlement. He was 17 on his first visit in 1946 and soon joined the youth club where he made many lasting friendships. There were two clubs, one for girls and one for boys, 'and they'd merge in the last half-hour. I retained my interest in the Settlement and, when I returned from National Service, I'd always drop in. In those days I'd grown a bit of a thirst for the golden nectar and I'd pop over for pint in "The Barrel". In its time the Settlement provided digs for university students – and later on I was one of two members invited to Sweden. About 15 years ago, former members met up at a reunion which was just like turning back the clock. The one-time youngsters had become prosperous adults.'

Gillian Brown nee Vinter lived at the Settlement between 1957 and 1960 when she was a full-time health visitor at Greet and Tyseley. She helped with the Saturday morning under 7 club and recalls trips to the pantomime and Christmas parties as well outings to Kinver where the Settlement had a camping site. At that time, Maureen White was the Girls' Club leader.

When Tripe was Great: Tripe and Onion and Faggots and Peas

She darted a look at the clock on the mantelpiece and then shifted her face to the young lad stretched out on the squab. Just for a few seconds she let her eyes linger on him and she couldn't help but smile. With his nose almost burrowed in the Wizard, she knew he was worlds away from Brum. He'd already saved England from foreign spies, and now he was about to hit the goal which would send his team to victory in the FA Cup. But he never got the chance. His mom's words ended his daydreams. 'Come on, ma lad. Get cracking. Y're dad'll be um soon and y'know how he always likes his tea on the table ready fer him. Let's be having y'.'

He knew better than to push it any further. Reluctantly he went into the scullery to get the white two-pint jug. When he came back into the house, his mom handed him a few coins and with the words 'no messing about' chasing him, the youngster set off down the road. The shop was only a hop, skip and a jump away, and when he got there he had to join a long queue. It seemed as if the same faces were there every week. There were old grannies with their black shawls pulled tightly around their shoulders, middle-aged women in their wrap-over pinnies and loads of kids like him sent out to fetch the tripe and onions for the old man.

It was a good five and twenty minutes before he got inside the door. The counter went down the middle of the place, not across it, and from the other side steam billowed from big metal tureens. Even though he'd watched it scores of times, it still remained a fascinating scene. As someone gave their order – perhaps it was half a pound of tripe or even a pound – the gaffer'd take hold of a long two-pronged fork and thrust it downwards into the boiling food. Swiftly he'd skewer a piece of tripe and bring it up, and then with a long knife he'd cut off the amount he wanted.

The tripe dealer always weighed the meat, putting it in a metal dish on one side of the scales – not that he should have bothered 'as he had a knack of cutting off almost the exact weight you wanted. Then he'd pierce the crinkly, white tripe again and push it into the jug of the customer. Finally he'd go back to the tureen and with a ladle he'd scoop up a load of juice and onions and pour them over the meat.

That was the one good thing about this errand. They always gave you plenty of the clear, broth-like liquid and that meant you could sip some of it on your way home! By the time you got back your taste buds were tingling, and you couldn't wait to get a piece with marge and dip it in the juice. He did that run every other week, 'cus in between he fetched the old man faggots and peas from another shop.

Funny how you always had to go for certain things to certain places. He always took the jug there as well, although he never knew how the old lady who ran the place coped the way she did. Her shop was just the front room of a house, and she did the cooking in the back kitchen. Where she lived in the house was a mystery, 'cus there couldn't have been much room, but any road she made bostin faggots.

She didn't open every night, just towards the weekend, but she must have knocked out hundreds of faggots. Made them all herself, too. She chopped up pounds and

Bradshaw's Dining Rooms are the focal point of this photograph of Navigation Street in the latter 1800s. Perhaps the most famous dining house ptoprietor in Birmingham in this period and into the early twentieth century was Mrs Mountford, whose premises were on the Bell Street end of the old Market Hall in the Bull Ring. Mrs Mountford was a large lady and she made a lasting impression on Jack Drasey of Stratford-upon-Avon when he was a boy. He is related to the Mountfords who ran a cooked meat shop in the Bull Ring. The original shop opened for fish and chips in Bell Street 'and Mrs Mountford kept her baby in a basket under the counter. After she'd made her money there, she opened up in the Bull Ring on the site where Woolworth's stood later'.

And what a fine sight this big woman was with her white coat, her gold fob watch and white apron! When she got even richer, she'd arrive from her Sutton Coldfield home, delighting in being noticed. Jack stresses that 'she was a show- woman, standing benevolently over steaming joints of pork, beef and lamb that stood on huge hot plates in her window, all ready to be served at noon. But she was good-hearted too. Many's the tramp who's been given a free sandwich and told not to come back again – but she knew they would and never refused them a bite. Then, the carving over, she'd sit by her till like a queen. Men would tap on the window, stick five fingers in the air to signify they'd be back for their lunches in five minutes and she'd have them ready. You got a smashing plateful of meat, two veg and potatoes for 6d.'

My own granddad and his brothers were grateful to Mrs Mountford. Like many other poor kids, they would forage a tanner of their mom and buy a quire of Mails – twelve newspapers. For that the Mail would chuck in one for free. They'd flog each paper for a ha'penny and when they'd sold the twelve they'd got their money back for their mom. The ha'penny from the thirteenth Mail was their own. With that they would go to Mrs Mountford's and buy a ha'penny dip – a piece dipped in the fat of the meat which was cooking in the window. Many's the time Mrs Mountford gave them and other poor kids a piece for nothing.

Josie Smith has sent in this cracking photo of Mrs June Tomlinson with her daughters Jenny and Doris and their dog Patch outside their cooked meat shop in Cattel Road, Small Heath at the time of coronation of King George V in 1911.

Pat Gumbley recalls that her husband's aunt, Irene Gumbley, ran cooked meat shops in Birmingham at the start of the twentieth century, one of them in Aston, opposite the Hippodrome. The family lived on the premises and did their own cooking of meats. Customers would leave carrying steaming hot pigs' feet wrapped in greaseproof. They'd eat them during performances and leave the bones under the seats. Irene herself had the job 'of burning the hairs off the trotters and pulling out the nails'.

Eileen Terry has never forgotten Cissie Robotham who 'would stand in the front of her shop window in Stratford Road, just past the junction with Showell Green Lane. There, against a backdrop of cooked meats, she had one eye on carving and one on passers-by – and she wielded her knife like a surgeon. She wore bright red lipstick, the sign of a fast woman in those days. But even better remembered was her glossy black hair, worn in a bob with a 'Claudette Colbert' fringe. It intrigued me because it seemed to be stuck to her forehead, and its ends were curled into a row of commas! From time to time, she'd acknowledge a regular with a wave of her knife. I loved going there with my mother for meat for tea or for my father's work sandwiches; no company canteens those days'.

Frank Scott's coffee rooms at 155, Montgomery Street, Sparkbrook at the turn of the twentieth century where you could get a hot dinner for just fourpence!

Waldrons of Pershore Road, Stirchley, was run by the parents of Peggy Beiver. He did the cooking and 'and mother hand-carved. She was convinced meat didn't taste right if machine-sliced. Customers would bring jugs to carry away gravy when they collected meat – and they'd ask for pies to be cut up so they could ea t them while downing a pint or two at the 'British Oak' pub just a few doors up. They were happy days.'

pounds of pork and liver, boiling it all up with onions, herbs and breadcrumbs and seasoning it with salt and pepper. When that was done, she'd roll the mixture into balls and to keep them moist she'd surround them with parts of the kell – the lacy, waxy lining of a pig's stomach. Then she baked the faggots in a great old black-leaded range, covering them in water. When the cooking was done, she added cornflower to the liquid and made a dark tasty gravy. And as for the much peas, well, she'd soaked a load of dry peas overnight and then boiled them before she opened up.

There were so many places to go for smashing faggots and peas, from Robbo's Café in Park Lane, Aston, to Mrs Landon of Ladywood. And where better for tripe and onions than Garry's of Cattell Road, Small Heath; Hanslow's off Foundry Road, Handsworth; Meredith's of Summer Lane; and Suckling's of Oldfield Road, Sparkbrook? They may all have gone from the streets of Brum, but their tastes linger on.